VOICES IN THE PURPLE HAZE

Underground Radio and the Sixties

MICHAEL C. KEITH

 PRAEGER

Westport, Connecticut
London

Library of Congress Cataloging-in-Publication Data

Keith, Michael C., date.
    Voices in the purple haze : underground radio and the sixties /
Michael C. Keith ; foreword by Dusty Street.
        p.   cm.—(Media and society series, ISSN 0890–7161)
    Includes bibliographical references and index.
    ISBN 0–275–95266–5 (alk. paper)
    1. Alternative radio broadcasting—United States—History—20th
century.   2. Subculture—United States—History—20th century.
3. United States—Social conditions—1960–1980.   I. Title.
II. Series.
HE8697.75.U6K45   1997
384.54—DC21   96–47247

British Library Cataloguing in Publication Data is available.

Library of Congress Catalog Card Number: 96–47247
ISBN: 0–275–95266–5
ISSN: 0890–7161

First published in 1997

Praeger Publishers, 88 Post Road West, Westport, CT 06881
An imprint of Greenwood Publishing Group, Inc.

Printed in the United States of America

The paper used in this book complies with the
Permanent Paper Standard issued by the National
Information Standards Organization (Z39.48–1984).

10 9 8 7 6 5 4 3 2 1

I want to be Galileo
And Sail through the sky
Know the stars as they are
And bathe in their why
Let Earth and its systems
Be what they will be
Revolve, evolve
I will move to be free.
                    —*Marion Wrye*

I am a child of Amerika
I love to listen to the radio.
                    —*Jerry Rubin*

We must rethink all our old ideas
and beliefs before they capture
and destroy us.
                    —*Robert F. Kennedy*

Contents

Foreword

How did it happen that I became the so-called First Lady
of commercial underground radio? Well, let me tell you . . .

I was a student at San Francisco State, and I took some acid one day and
decided that being a student wasn't what I wanted to do. So after a year in
the classroom, I went to Mexico. When I came back in 1967, I saw this guy
on the street, whom I had met while at school, and I told him that I didn't
know what I wanted to do. He said they just started this radio station called
KMPX, and they were looking for female engineers. I quickly responded
that I didn't know a damn thing about radio. He said, "Sure you do, and you
can always lie."

So that is what I did. I met Tom Donahue, and I told him that I had a
license and knew how to engineer. He told me he would get back to me. He
called three months later, and, in the summer of 1967, I started as an
engineer at KMPX, knowing nothing at all about the business.

I made horrible mistakes the first day I was at the station. My mistakes
were so bad that the on-air disc jockey, Bob Prescott, told me to go home
and think about the whole thing before I came back. I was so humiliated
that I returned that night and asked the all-night jock what to do. I stayed
until my shift the next day, and when Bob came in I knew enough to get by.
It was just a process of getting to know the audio board and equipment, and
what buttons to push and which ones to leave alone. I pretty much learned
by doing.

All the engineers were women—young girls, actually. I was Dusty
"Super Chic" Street, and the others were Suzie Cream Cheese and Katy

"The Easter Pig" Johnson. I don't know why Katy's middle name was "the Easter Pig."

So it happened that I met this man named Vaco Cash, who was a record producer and also on the air weekends. He had this bizarre show—a combination of every kind of music. It was truly an eclectic, freeform show with these great leaps from one music genre to another. He somehow made it all work, and I became his engineer. I fell madly in love with his musical taste, and he and I became really good friends.

Then we decided that the ladies should be able to get on the air because we really kept the place operating. They gave us a show that I think was called "The Chicks on Sunday" or something weird like that. Anyway, it was Raechel Donahue (Raechel Hamilton then), Buzzy Donahue (Tom Donahue's daughter), and the three female engineers, and we pretty much did our own thing on Sunday. After we (KMPX) went on strike because the station tried to fire our leader, Tom Donahue, we ended up at a different radio station, KSAN, run by Metromedia. Thinking back, that was probably the only time that an entire radio staff who was on strike stayed intact to ride the airwaves at another station in the same town.

Unfortunately, KSAN was a combo operation, meaning that the deejays had to run their own board. Luckily for me, Vaco was a producer as well as a very bizarre fellow, and while we were on strike, I became his assistant recording engineer. So I went back with him and did his shows. He was kind of anti-magnetic, and he couldn't really get the gist of running his own radio show, so he needed me. I was pretty much his gofer and Girl Friday, as I was when he was producing records. I'd go around with him when he'd do albums and keep track of everything. I'm not really sure what I did, but I did something.

Well, he got really sick one night and couldn't make his show. So Tom Donahue called me up and said that since I was the only one who knew Vaco's music, I'd be his fill-in, which I was. This won me a weekend slot. Tom took credit for my discovery, since he was the one who first put me on the air. That's how my career started.

I did weekends for about six months. A guy named Roland Young, who was this very militant black deejay, did 10:00 to 2:00 weeknights, at a time when the Black Panthers were at the very height of their visibility. We were working for Metromedia, so when one of the company's bigwigs visiting San Francisco heard Roland quote Panther David Hilliard on the air saying, "I will take the life of the President or anyone who stands in the way of my freedom," things got hot, and Roland got the ax. With that, they put me on full-time. That was in 1969, and I was working 10:00 at night until 2:00 in the morning doing rock 'n' roll radio for KSAN. I was there for four or five years.

It was really interesting because I truly was the first one on the air. There were no female engineers. I think there had been one or two ladies on the air. In other incarnations, there was Mother Coight (or Coyt), who lasted a short time. Turned out, it was really Gale Garnett, who sang the hit "We'll Sing in the Sunshine," and there was Allison Steele back East.

At any rate, in San Francisco, and I do believe on the whole West Coast, I was it for a good couple of years. It was an extraordinary experience, one that I go into in great detail in my book, *Fly Low and Avoid the Radar: The Adventures of Dangerous Dusty Street.*

I really got a lot of support from the guys. I find that there is a lot more suppression of women today than there was in the late 1960s and early 1970s. All of the guys that I worked with just related to me like I was one of the team. I was just one of the gang, and they were all there to help me. There was no male chauvinism, and there was equal pay for equal work.

We did form our own union, so that kept things pretty equitable and fair. It was called something like the United Progressive Underground FM Radio Workers of the Planet. Anyway, everything was equal in those days, and it was great because I had the reputation for doing a very bluesy show. I did not play the same music as everyone else. I got a lot of great press in those days, and it wasn't because I was a female disc jockey. It was because of the music I was playing, and probably because I was the only one on the radio, outside of the black radio stations, doing so. Other radio stations had playlists that were really Top 40, but I had the freedom to play the stuff I wanted to, which was R&B and the so-called race music of the day. I spun a lot of Aretha Franklin, Sam and Dave, and Bobby Blue.

I became the darling of every minor independent record promoter, and a lot of cool people came and hung out with me. I started to get a lot of interviews, which is where I honed a lot of my interview talents. When I listen to them today, I sound like one of those stoned little hippie chicks, and, well, that's what I was. Yes, it was a time when there were a lot of mind-altering chemicals around. I, of course, did my fair share, keeping up with everybody else. I think because I worked at night, I felt that I could do more and be more creative with the aid of drugs. I also felt pressure to keep fending off fatigue.

San Francisco was a crazy place to be back then, and being in underground radio there made it even crazier. We were the darlings of the town and had tons of fun and hung out with the Grateful Dead, Dr. John, Janis Joplin, and all the rest. We were pretty much that little hippie family, that movement that everyone talks about. If you were on the radio, you were a part of the music scene, and super producers, like Bill Graham, were a part of the radio station.

You know, nothing's perfect. It's a hassle just being a puppy, as I often said on the air—quoting from a favorite Sylvester cartoon—but those days and those radio shows were something pretty unique and special.

In *Voices in the Purple Haze* you can get a real good sense of the whole wicked trip. So read on and, of course, try to feel the groove!

Dusty Street

Preface

───■

> Isn't it just groovy what you can hear on the radio these days?
>
> —Tiny Tim

In 1966, as the country rocked from widespread social unrest, commercial radio went underground to do some rocking of its own. Thus began the brief but glorious life span of one of the audio medium's most remarkable programming genres.

A multitude of unique factors contributed to the rise of commercial underground (also known as freeform, alternative, and progressive) radio, and *Voices in the Purple Haze* sets out to examine them through the perspectives of some of the format's foremost practitioners.

The book has been designed primarily as an oral history—a memoir or family album, if you will—of the commercial underground radio phenomenon, which was as much a product of the turbulent times as it was a reaction to the numbing status quo prevalent in the broadcast industry.

Over two dozen underground pioneers—this book's "Voices"—reflect on the nature, evolution, and, ultimately, the demise, of their unique brand of radio—sometimes labeled "hippie" radio by less than friendly critics. The "Voices" (list follows Preface) that drive the narrative are integrated throughout the book. They engage in a conversation, a dialogue, on what may arguably be radio's most extraordinary post-television manifestation. These contributors offer a kaleidoscope of impressions, anecdotes, and views in what might strike the reader as a sort of magical mystery tour of a time when radio was very different indeed. In addition to the words from the "horse's mouth," published opinions of some of the prominent social, political, and cultural commentators on the era are incorporated for the sake of enhanced context.

This book seeks to illuminate and inform its readers (albeit in its own unorthodox way) about a subject upon which little has been written to date. It is the first book-length oral history on the commercial underground airwaves. Texts and individual accounts have been published on specific radio stations and careers, among them Susan Krieger's *Hip Capitalism*, Steve Post's *Playing in the FM Band*, and Jim Ladd's *Radio Waves*, but no single volume has offered an overall assessment of the medium—what it was, why it was the way it was, and why it perished.

Many individuals have contributed their time and talent to the making of this book. Among those who certainly warrant acknowledgment are J. Fred MacDonald, Joe Beaton, Carla Brooks Johnston, Lee Nadel, Donna Halper, Lynn Christian, John Katsulas, Robert Hilliard, Fred Hill, and Susanne Riette-Keith. At the top of this list, of course, are those who serve as the book's heart and soul—its "Voices." It is to these former underground broadcasters and astute media observers that this text is dedicated. It is their story and, for many, a return trip to their fondest professional and personal experiences.

It is important to note that there are many underground stations, pioneers, and practitioners not cited in these pages. Their voices have not been included either because they chose not to participate in this retrospective or because their whereabouts were unknown a quarter century after underground radio's departure from the airwaves. In either case, they too deserve to be saluted for their participation in one of commercial radio's stellar moments.

The Voices

———————————————————————————————■

LEE ABRAMS: Former head of rock programming for ABC Radio and one of the country's foremost radio consultants. Principal architect of the album-oriented rock format.

DAN CARLISLE: Deejay during underground era at legendary Detroit station WABX-FM. On-air personality at WNEW-FM and KLOS-FM and a half dozen other stations.

DAVE DIXON: Deejay during underground era at WABX-FM in Detroit. Longtime broadcaster.

RAECHEL DONAHUE: Chief cohort and widow of underground radio pioneer Tom Donahue. Staff member at KMPX-FM and KSAN-FM in San Francisco. Currently a voice performer in motion pictures and television.

DWIGHT DOUGLAS: Prominent radio programming consultant and broadcaster in early FM rock format.

BEN FONG-TORRES: Disc jockey at legendary underground station KSAN-FM and former editor of *Rolling Stone*. Presently managing editor of *The Gavin*.

JOHN GEHRON: Early FM rock broadcaster. Currently chief operating officer of American Radio Systems.

RUSS GIBB: Disc jockey at pioneer underground rocker WABX-FM and Top 40 deejay at WKMH-FM, Detroit.

JOHN GORMAN: Head of operations for Cleveland's longtime top FM rocker, WMMS-FM.

SHELLEY GRAFMAN: Vice president and general manager of early St. Louis underground station KSHE-FM.

MIKE HARRISON: Early underground broadcaster and currently publisher of *Talkers* magazine.

ROBERT HILLIARD: Chief, Educational (Public) Broadcasting Branch of the Federal Communications Commission from 1961 to 1980.

KATE INGRAM: Member of programming staff at KSAN-FM. Presently programmer at KUSF-FM.

ROLAND JACOPETTI: Production director during underground heyday of KSAN-FM.

CARLA BROOKS JOHNSTON: President, New Century Policies, writing and consulting on public policy and the media.

CHARLES LAQUIDARA: Deejay at pioneer underground station KPPC in Pasadena, California. Boston's foremost FM rock radio personality for thirty years at WBCN and WZLX.

LARRY MILLER: Original underground deejay and programmer at KMPX-FM and WABX-FM.

SCOTT MUNI: Preeminent FM rock personality at New York's first underground radio stations, WOR-FM and WNEW-FM.

ALLEN MYERS: Media analyst for the Federal Communications Commission.

SCOOP NISKER: Pioneer news reporter and producer during KSAN-FM's underground era.

THOM O'HAIR: Early 1970s program director at KSAN-FM. Announcer, music director, and manager at a dozen radio stations. Concert and record promoter.

DAVE PIERCE: Pioneer deejay and music director for KPPC-FM. Stage and screen actor and television station account executive.

STEFAN PONEK: Underground deejay and onetime program director at KSAN-FM.

TIM POWELL: Early music director and programmer at underground stations, including WABX, KMPX, and KLOS.

BOBBY SEALE: Founder and Chairman of the Black Panther Party. Director of REACH.

ED SHANE: Program director of Atlanta's pioneer underground station, WPLO-FM. National program consultant and president of Shane Media.

ALLEN SHAW: President of ABC-FM owned radio stations and innovator of the network's syndicated progressive "Love" format. Currently president of Crescent Communications.

BONNIE SIMMONS: Music librarian and programmer at KSAN-FM during underground days.

LARRY SOLEY: Prominent author and educator. Professor of Communications at Marquette University.

DUSTY STREET: Pioneer female deejay in underground radio. Member of air staff at KSAN-FM. Presently a deejay in Las Vegas.

AL WILSON: Early Detroit underground radio practitioner. Former manager of East Lansing's "Edge-FM."

FRANK WOOD: Founder of Cincinnati's first underground radio station, WEBN-FM. Currently president of Secret Communications.

KSAN poster depicting Tom Donahue and his crew.

Chapter One

Murmurs of the Rebel Yell

Music power at the tower of hits, hits, hits . . .

"How many goddamn times can you play Herman's Hermits and still feel good about what you do?" lamented Tom Donahue, aloud and to himself, in the spring of 1966. The man who would ultimately be credited with conceiving the antidote to the toxic patter and yalp of Top 40 had achieved much of his own success in that very radio format, but now he had hit the proverbial wall. He could not, and would not, spin another inane doowop chart-climber. Something had to give. Radio was in for some much needed shock therapy.

Big Daddy, as Tom Donahue was nicknamed because of his softly commanding presence on the air and his 400-pound torso, was contemplating a whole new kind of radio—maybe an expanded version of the quirky all-night show hosted by deejay Larry Miller on a little-known Bay Area FMer called KMPX, or perhaps something that emulated the appealing insouciance found on the noncommercial end of the band.

Anything would be better than the pump and drivel of Top 40, the scourge of the audio medium, "the rotting corpse, stinking up the airways."[1]

SATORI IN A NEBRASKA BAR

Number one, one, one . . . on wonderful WINO. . .

Legend has it that Top 40 radio was conceived by a couple of young broadcasters while they commiserated over drinks at a favorite watering hole in Omaha in 1955. Todd Storz and Bill Stewart had been anything but successful running KOWH. In fact, out of six stations in the market, they would joke about being number seven on those days when there was nothing left to do but make light about their gloomy circumstances.

The medium of radio itself was slowly recovering from its fall from grace with the American public. The early 1950s were anything but joyous times for the first electronic mass medium. It was a time of deep reflection and regrouping following a near knockout blow by what was ironically called sightradio or radiovision by many who were not yet comfortable with the term "television."

Several things would contribute to radio's rehabilitation and eventual revival. Bell Laboratory scientists had made possible miniaturization, or the downsizing of radio receivers, with their creation of the transistor. This made the medium more mobile and companionable. A radio could be taken on a stroll in the park or on a romp at the beach without incurring muscle strain. Portable radios prior to the transistor were anything but portable.

Another factor contributing to radio's renewal and rebirth was the plan of the Federal Communications Commission (FCC) to localize the medium through the allocation of regional (nonmetropolitan) frequencies. Up to World War II, radio was primarily a network-driven, large-market enterprise, and the FCC felt that it could better serve the American public if it were available on a community-by-community basis. Thus, radio became a more personal experience for the listener.

> *Carla Brooks Johnston:* Ultimately, this localization decision would coincide perfectly with the availability of the empowered sixties generation. Drawing on their "can-do" parents' belief that anything is possible, and driven by their own anger about shattered dreams, these young people saw no problem in recreating radio in their own image.

The situation was further enhanced when radio programmers woke up to the reality that they had to approach their sought-after clientele—the audience and advertisers—in a different way than they had previously. The result of this slow-to-emerge recognition was the concept of program specialization. Stations would break with the tradition of attempting to attract five- to fifty-year-olds and set their sights on a specific segment of the listening population. They would target what they perceived as a potentially desirable age group (in ratings parlance, a demographic) to prospective sponsors.

In order to accomplish this objective, it was necessary to air the sounds—namely, music—most appealing to an intended audience. The first manifestations of this concept appeared in the form of classical, country, and popular music radio, as well as something cryptically referred to as middle-of-the-road, which tended to play the standards of the day and a little bit of everything else deemed broadly acceptable and inoffensive.

ROCK AROUND THE CLOCK

Movin' and a-cruisin' and havin' a ball . . .

Pop radio of the early 1950s meant the three Bs—ballads, big band, and boogie woogie—but in the middle of the decade another musical genre, something completely new to most listeners, would shatter the standard alliterative approach to the second coming of the aural medium with one of its own. It would be known as rock and roll.

By the time Storz and Stewart had concluded that by playing the songs people would spend their hard-earned money to hear, Bill Haley and His Comets were on their way to recording history with the first million-selling rock and roll single, "Rock Around the Clock."

In a matter of months, rock and roll records were outselling all other types, and the hit music format conceived by a couple of desperate broadcasters (necessity being the mother of invention) on a gloomy day in Omaha was drawing a predominantly youthful audience. Kids were the primary consumers of the new pulse-throbbing rhythms, and they were a buying force with which to be reckoned. The decade characterized by McCarthyism, the Cold War, and the grand migration of the silent generation and their baby-boomer offspring to the suburbs interestingly became the backdrop for the introduction of the primal beat, which would inspire suspicion and fear in many parents and adults, while planting the seeds of unrest and rebellion in their progeny. Radio was there to both stir the surf and ride the waves.

Robert Hilliard: This is true to a degree. For example, while resistance to McCarthyism was virtually nonexistent on commercial radio stations, the noncommercial Pacifica stations did have the gumption to reflect the attitudes of the relatively few Americans who took an overt stand against the country's incipient fascism. In fact, in the early 1950s, I remember searching in vain to hear the anti-McCarthy satirical record, "The Investigator," on U.S. radio. I recall listening to it on a Canadian station that reached

New York after dusk. I was able to buy the record—which had no identification of producer or performers—at one of the few "progressive" bookstores left in New York. This wasn't a disc you were about to hear on any mainstream station, especially not chart stations. Although the music being offered by some stations was from a new direction, that was about all that was new. Everything else was still rigid establishment.

Chart radio (Top 40) in 1956 was a different animal than its original incarnation little more than a year before on the Storz station in the country's heartland. Rock and roll singles, called forty-fives (a recording innovation of the period), would help pave the path from the traditional crooners and balladeers of the day (such as Vaughn Monroe and Eddie Fisher) to a new breed of recording artists like Chuck Berry, Elvis Presley, Fats Domino, and Jerry Lee Lewis.

Affordable to young people, the 45 rpm record was the perfect purveyor of the finger-snapping doowop ditties being produced and packaged in multitudes by legions of established and aspiring recording companies, which relied on the growing number of hit music stations to provide the necessary exposure for their product. Thus, a perfect union was formed between the medium that produced the song and the medium that played it. Radio and the recording industry were married under the sign of the dollar, and the couple have lived a remarkably prosperous, if not occasionally stormy, existence ever since.

SPINNING THE HITS

Where the Good Guys groove to today's top tunes . . .

Top 40 . . . Top 30 . . . Top 20 . . . Top 10. Narrow playlists were the game plan. Simply stated, pop chart stations aired the songs that sold the most. That was the quintessential philosophy that drove these stations, and repetition of the hit tunes was the strategy they employed. The bigger the song, the more airplay it received. When an artist (Elvis) or group (Beatles) was hot, it dominated a station. Megahits were spun until they were threadbare.

Short cuts (two-and-a-half minute selections were standard) were a primary ingredient of the frenetic programming formula, and recording companies worked hand in hand with pop chart stations to make certain that the system hummed like a well-maintained cash register.

Underground radio guru Tom Donahue remarked shortly after departing the all-hits format:

> [It] aimed its message directly at the lowest common denominator. The disc jockeys have become robots performing their inanities at the direction of programmers who have succeeded in totally squeezing the human element out of their sound, reducing it to a series of blips and bleeps and happy, yes, always happy, sounding cretins who are poured from bottles every three hours.[2]

Donahue was not the format's only critic. Nearly everyone outside of Top 40 had disparaging things to say about radio's leading youth audience grabber. The views of Mike Gormley in the *Detroit Free Press* were typical:

> If there is one second of silence, meaning no commercial, no yelling disc jockeys or no Melanie singing "Lay Down," all hell breaks loose in the boss' office. . . . The on-air people at AM stations are not allowed to sound like themselves. They are very seldom allowed to even have their own given-at-birth names.[3]

Top 40 deejays had to sound like Top 40 deejays, which meant yelling and screaming things they believed the teens tuned in would regard as hip and with it. The best Top 40 personalities, from Alan Freed to Cousin Brucie, and even Tom Donahue, achieved a sacred, often herolike status among their young followers. They were the personification of cool, and for this they were celebrated and lavishly compensated.

> *Tim Powell:* These guys dominate my memory of radio when I was a kid, especially Tom Donahue. He had a big following. I remember him best. He'd say, "I'm here to clear up your face and mess up your mind." These guys tried to relate within the confines of what they were doing, and there were confines.

Doowop sound bites were accompanied by echo chambered, high-intensity chatter and goofy giveaways, anything from a "W-Amazing-B-C" wall banner to a ticket for the Coney Island parachute drop. Newscasts and public service programs were a required part of radio during the format's heyday, but these would be modified and altered to match the hyperkinetic flow of sounds.

For instance, news was regarded as a tuneout factor ("Kids don't want it!"), so usually it was dealt with like a hot coal and thrown away in a rapid-fire rush of sensational headlines intermingled with sound effects and commercials about pimple cures. Public service programs could and would be buried on Sunday mornings (the "dead zone"), when no self-respecting adolescent could be found in a conscious state.

ROCK 'N' ROLL's RADIO BAND

Hug your baby tight and tune this tune to the top.

The standard broadcast band, as AM was officially called, was the initial home of rock music and Top 40. FM radios were barely available. Less than 5 percent of all radios in the United States were FM in the mid-1950s, as Top 40 and rock and roll were being launched.

Nearly ten years later things had not changed a great deal in this regard, although rock music had entered another phase, principally heralded by the British invasion.

Tim Powell: Around 1965 there were damn few FM stations even on the air anywhere in the country. FM had been around for thirty-plus years and stereo FM for a decade or so, but there were only about 600 stations on the static-free band. There were maybe about 50 to 75 construction permits in the works to put new FMs on the air, but things were slow. In those days the FCC was not as uptight about making the holders of CPs build. You could string it out for a while, sometimes for years. Not many of the stations on the air (or planned) were broadcast in stereo. About 5 percent or so of the audience owned any type of FM receiver, let alone stereo. Hell, the LP was barely a decade old and was primarily pressed in mono. Around that time you could get a stereo version of some albums, but it cost you more. About the only person who had a stereo, and everybody had a friend or uncle like this, was some nut who had built his own stereo and played you records that featured trains and jets swooshing from right to left speaker and back again. What a yawn. AM radio ruled, and the rebel station on the edge of town and at the top of the dial played rock and roll. The cool stations were Top 40, with catchy jingles and jocks who talked up to the very start of the vocal. The tempo was in step with the powerful V-8 engines of the day, which gulped obscene quantities of 25 cents a gallon high test gasoline with lotsa lead in it. The twin Smithys sang along with the reverb rear speakers. Bras crossed her heart, and you hoped to cross that line. Life was good. Lucky Strikes were around 50 cents a pack, and you didn't have a clue that they would kill you. And the radio played on.

These were, indeed, the "happy days" for AM radio, which had success-fully survived a near deadly attack by the enfant terrible—television. FM was "nowhere, man," as far as the kids were concerned. It was "egghead" radio, the place where squares would tune to hear opera and other artsy-fartsy stuff. AM was the place to be, where the cool cats spoke in a language teens understood and in a language by which parents seemed oddly threat-ened and disturbed.

Little changed in the tone and tenor of AM Top 40 music playlists from the format's early days to its twelfth birthday mark, despite the fact that considerable change had occurred in American society and culture. A

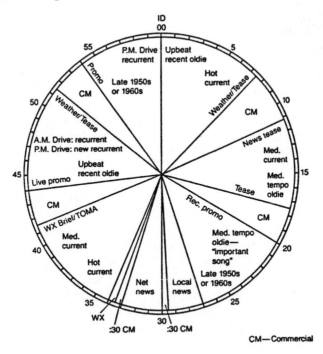

A highly structured and congested program clock of a mainstream pop music radio station.

comparison of some pop chart station favorites of 1957–1959 with those of 1967–1969 bears this out:

1957–1959	**1967–1969**
Elvis Presley, "All Shook Up"	American Breed, "Bend Me, Shape Me"
Pat Boone, "Love Letters in the Sand"	
The Del-Vikings, "Come Go with Me"	Cowsills, "Indian Lake"
The Everly Brothers, "Wake Up, Little Susie"	Association, "Windy"
	Herman's Hermits, "Kind of a Hush"
Paul Anka, "Diana"	Monkees, "Daydream Believer"
The Silhouettes, "Get a Job"	Ohio Express, "Yummy, Yummy"
Bobby Darin, "Splish Splash"	Jay & the Americans, "Magic Moment"
Richie Valens, "Donna"	Glen Campbell, "Wichita Lineman"
The Crests, "16 Candles"	Archies, "Sugar, Sugar"

DESCENDING THE TOP 40

> Come on, and go, go, go,
> with Cousin Brucie.
> Go, go, go, go, go, go . . .

Top 40 stations continued to rely on the tried and true two-and-a-half-minute single even as rock music was evolving and maturing with albums that often featured lengthier cuts with more complex rhythms and messages.

Tim Powell: None of the formats on the AM band played any real album tracks in the rock arena. In Los Angeles in the mid-1960s, several Top 40 stations played "Going Home" from the Rolling Stones' *Aftermath* LP around midnight. That was pretty avante garde for them. The overnight jock on KYA-AM played Ray Charles' "The Right Time" at midnight to open his show in the early 1960s. Undoubtedly there were album tracks heard on AM Top 40 stations, but it was an aberrant event, not a central or routine piece of programming.

Raechel Donahue: You know, most of us from that era were tuning Top 40. We were kids and we were into pop rock, but as the music became more sophisticated and said more than "I Wanna Hold Your Hand," we began to drift away. Tom was fed up with bubblegum, head-candy radio. There was so much else happening in rock that was ignored by radio. It really was a "rotting corpse," as he wrote in *Rolling Stone*.

Allen Shaw: It was pretty stale by the mid-1960s, I'd have to agree. But looking back you can appreciate that Top 40 was very innovative at its inception. It broke away from convention, just as underground did a decade later. It was a new form of radio at the time, and it kind of operated by the seat of its pants. Guys like Todd Storz, Gordon McLendon, Bill Drake, and others were experimenters in their own right. Initially, in Top 40, there was quite a bit of latitude given to deejays. There was some freedom. It became rigid later on, and that is when it calcified. Of course, this opened the door for the next wave of youth-oriented formats.

That many of Top 40's prominent practitioners were among the first to grow weary, as well as wary, of the programming formula and to long for something more substantive and meaningful makes sense, considering what was happening in rock music and culture at the time.

Raechel Donahue: These were people who were out there and knew what was going on in music and in youth society. Tom knew better than most what was happening, and he knew Top 40 wasn't, at least not for him and many others.

Donahue expressed his distaste for Top 40 nearly every chance he got, and eventually he became one of its most ardent and vocal critics.

[Rock music] has matured, the audience has matured, but radio has apparently proven to be a retarded child. Where once Top 40 radio reflected the taste of its audience, today it attempts to dictate it, and in the process has alienated its once loyal army of listeners.[4]

Mike Gormley, who wrote frequently on electronic media, expressed the sentiments of many, including Donahue, in a 1970 article: "It's now up to FM stations to try new things, to invent new ways of doing old things and, well—experiment."[5] Looking back at the exodus of some Top 40 programmers, the industry's foremost trade publication, *Broadcasting*, noted:

The most prominent practitioners of progressive rock are refugees from Top 40 who so strongly felt the need to reject the musical and personal values of AM rock that they separated themselves from Top 40 by saying what they were not (AM, that is) instead of presenting an image of what they were.[6]

The time was ripe for change. As President Kennedy stated so eloquently and presciently in his 1961 inaugural address, "Let the word go forth from this time and place, to friend and foe alike, that the torch has been passed to a new generation of Americans."

CHANGE IN THE AIR

Radio just plain stunk. There were two minute doowops with hyper-thyroidal deejays up and down the dial. Something new was desperately needed.

—Dave Fonras, 1966

If the start of the 1950s was perceived as a time of general optimism born of a sense that nothing but better days lay ahead for most Americans, the early 1960s were viewed with a bit less certitude, if not uneasiness. These were years when the future of the country did not look quite as rosy to everyone in the comfortable mainstream. The future did, however, appear infinitely brighter to others—those legions less franchised and embraced by society. In fact, the so-called happy days of the first full post–World War II decade would prove to be the relative calm before the storm of subsequent ones.

Carla Brooks Johnston: The general optimism of the fifties was born in the heady days after the war—WWII. The boys won! The boys were home! And it was time to gather the trophies that marked the good life. No more public transportation; millions bought their first car. Farms were subsidized and suburbia was created. No need for the women to work anymore. "Rosie the Riveter" returned to the kitchen with the aid of a new Mixmaster and Betty Crocker mixes. She started her "Leave It to Beaver" family. These heady days of commercialism took on a new look in the early sixties. America elected its first Catholic president. Anything was possible. But, most important, the First Family was young, charismatic, and it was indeed Camelot. Meanwhile, the colored people of the forties and fifties also sought the postwar good life. Now as Negroes, they migrated by the thousands from the farms of the South to the cities of the North. Feeling the same optimism, Rosa Parks dared to sit in the front of a bus—defying the 1950s segregation laws. The courts had banned school desegregation. Equality was just around the corner. The postwar "Atoms for Peace" program provided a way to rationalize the horrors of atomic weaponry and a way for the scientists to keep their fascinating and lucrative experiments. Atmospheric testing was truly awesome. Some of the boys unlucky enough to be fifties vets were marched in front of these explosions—just an experiment in the name of science. America was promised electricity "too cheap to meter." It was all a dream.

Rock music and Top 40 radio helped keep the specter of the Atomic Age at bay for many young baby boomers, who lived comfortably in expanding suburbs with parents intent on giving them the kind of life that their own parents could only have imagined. But this seemingly idyllic lifestyle brought with it expectations and demands that fostered feelings of resentment, if not rebellion, in a growing number of young people.

Tim Powell: Being an American who was raised in the popular culture of black and white network television when Eisenhower was president is an experience underappreciated. It was like driving a tank and being under it at the same time. I have very little faith that anyone can put into words how the public was hammered into a unified, patriotic, hard-working, sexist, racist clump. It was truly a stultifying time. We weren't taught about McCarthyism or the Rosenbergs. The nations of Russia and China were un-places. Kids graduated from college, and they had no concept of the difference between Ivan the Terrible and Peter the Great. Politics conveniently erased things and places from lectures and textbooks. There were geographic Russias and Chinas, but no history, except that depicting the "hideous" nature of communism. There was a lockstep mentality that, at least on the surface, was standard American behavior. I didn't know what a homosexual was until I was 16 or 17. That's how different things were back then. "Ozzie and Harriet," "Leave It to Beaver," and "The Dick Van Dyke Show," while they wrap chronologically into later years, typify the unrealizable norm that was America in the 1950s and 1960s. The war against

Germany and Japan had pulled the U.S. out of the Depression of the 1930s. World War II was a defined war. While most wars end up having a hazy distinction between good and evil, World War II actually pitted decent behavior against the darkest evil seen since the Inquisition. The mind-set of "defeating evil" was American karma, or so it seemed. The soldiers came home, made lots of babies, and then cooked these kids in the stew of the quintessential American dream.

Some social critics have referred to this first postwar generation as "spoiled brats," arguing that parents of baby boomers overcompensated, giving their children what they themselves did not have in the lean and turbulent times in which they grew up. This, they contend, set the stage for the youth rebellion, since affluence and security were all but taken for granted. A growing number of young people did not share their parents' seemingly obsessive appetite for things of a material nature, or so they thought.

The placid, if not complacent, family setting, in which conformity was the rule rather than the exception, helped fuel interest in pop rock radio. Referring to the relationship between teens and their electronic companion, writer and social critic Tom Wolfe observed, "They use the radio as a background, the aural prop for whatever kind of life they want to imagine they're leading."[7]

Home was not the only place young people felt the repressive hand of authority. Escaping to college in the 1950s and early 1960s was not really escaping at all. Universities treated students like children. They assumed the role of surrogate parents—*in loco parentis*—keeping close tabs on the behavior of their young, not fully assimilated and indoctrinated charges.

> *Dusty Street:* This was probably one of the reasons I felt compelled to leave school and head off to Mexico. Of course, things were changing in the 1960s compared to the previous decade. They had to. Society was undergoing a massive realignment, or beginning one, and young people were an important element of this.

While rumblings of unrest emanated from the youth camp in the 1950s (Marlon Brando, James Dean, and Sal Mineo exemplified this in the "rebel" movies of the day, as did writers like Jack Kerouac and Allen Ginsberg, who composed anthems for the new Beat Generation), in great part, the decade could be characterized by the relative adherence of most young people to establishment values and dictates. For the most part, this was not the case with this same age group in the 1960s. Students became activists, protesting whatever they felt threatened by or detracted from the quality of their lives. Whether it be rigid administrative policies (college and governmental), the draft, or racial inequality, students were prepared to protest, and they did. By the mid-1960s there were 16 million cultural rebels, and most were under thirty years old. Things were turning upside down, and many young radio listeners were a part of this movement, one which would lead them to higher ground . . . underground.

> *Thom O'Hair:* Radio was now in the throes of the battle for the souls of America's youth. It had won one battle, and it was about to engage in another, which would be waged from a different direction.

NOTES

1. Tom Donahue, "Rotting Corpse," *Rolling Stone*, November 23, 1967, p. 2.

2. Mike Gormley, "WABX Is David, Knocking 'Em Dead with Rock," *Detroit Free Press*, August 9, 1970, p. 7.

3. Ibid.

4. Donahue, "Corpse," November 23, 1967.

5. Gormley, "WABX Is David," p. 7.

6. *Broadcasting*, September 24, 1973.

7. Tom Wolfe, *The Kandy-Kolored Tangerine-Flake Streamline Baby* (New York: Farrar, Straus and Giroux, 1965), p. 40.

Chapter Two

Seeding the Underground

The counterculture was a media event.
—Charles R. Morris

The subterranean rumblings of the 1950s culminated in the volcanic eruption that was the 1960s. The hot ash of change descended upon the nation, transforming the social and cultural landscape. The stage, replete with trapdoor to the underground, was in place. Social critics and scholars of the period have pointed out that the time was marked by a unique convergence of elements, an agglomeration seldom witnessed.

In a decade-end review of the 1960s, *Life* magazine called its images "violent, nostalgic, preposterous, maddening, amusing, sometimes immensely evocative and moving."[1]

For many, the catalytic element in this simmering caldron was the assassination of President Kennedy. Things would never be the same again, despaired a nation of shocked and bereaved mourners. Kennedy had inspired a renewed desire for change, a sense that all good and noble things were possible and attainable, but Camelot was gone, and what lay ahead more resembled Hades than the recent empyrean past. Further assassinations, racial upheaval, and an undeclared war were around the corner. All of these things, along with the growing use of mind-altering drugs, primarily by young people, contributed to the blossoming of the so-called counterculture.

Other things thickened the stew of the time. "Irrationalism, existential anxiety, the sheer numbers of adolescents with not much to do, all led to the blooming of the counterculture," noted Charles R. Morris in his study of the period, *A Time of Passion*.[2] In a more recent book, *The Movement and the Sixties*, Terry H. Anderson posits the widely held view that dissatisfaction with the political norm of the day seeded the clouds of dissent. "The counterculture must be defined broadly. The movement developed as a counter to the political establishment. The counterculture was a counter to the dominant cold war culture."[3]

> *Tim Powell:* Well, it was all that and more. There certainly was a large mass of young people milling about, so to speak. When these baby boomers hit their post-adolescence and early twenties, they went nuts. More properly stated, the burgeoning group of young people began to question everything and act everything out too. Because there were a lot of them, it was news enough in the new electronic age and good imagery for the film at eleven. Due to the ubiquitous nature of the media, even most rural areas knew about this bunch of people.

In one of the landmark publications on the 1960s, *The Making of the Counter Culture*, Theodore Roszak contends that the youth rebellion was born of what he explains as "a matter of machine tooling [of young people] to the needs of our various baroque bureaucracies: corporate, governmental, military, trade union, educational."[4] He continues:

> The young stand forth so prominently because they act against a background of nearly pathological passivity on the part of the adult generation. . . . The fact is, it is the young who have in their amateurish, even grotesque way, gotten dissent off the adult drawing board.[5]

Roszak goes on to argue that drugs played a key role in this disavowal by young people of adult society, while simultaneously leading them astray.

> Psychedelic experience participates significantly in the young's most radical rejection of the parental society. Yet it is their frantic search for the pharmacological panacea which tends to distract many of the young from all that is most valuable in their rebellion, and which threatens to destroy their most promising sensibilities.[6]

> *Carla Brooks Johnston:* Drugs played a part for some, and it became "in" to at least try drugs by the late sixties and early seventies. However, psychedelic drugs did not fuel the ferment of the civil rights movement or the women's movement or the ban the bomb movement or the environmental movement.

It all started with Larry Miller back at KMPX. Artwork by Larry Miller (1967).

Ultimately, a common cause solidified the youth movement in a way that threatened the status quo so cherished by the incumbent system. "A common composite enemy—the Vietnam War, racism, global imperialism—was the prime unifying force, leading to shared demonstrations and occupations," writes David Caute,[7] who defines counterculture as

> a term that embraces a plethora of disparate notions: dropout hippies, obscene language, acid trips, underground newspapers and films, alternative theatre with attendant "happenings," anti-universities, surreal street politics, communal self-help, folk and rock music alien to ears attuned to Beethoven or the Palm Court Orchestra, mystical cults, aggressive sexuality, flamboyant clothing, ecological awareness, rejection of ambition and careerism.[8]

As former underground radio deejay Jim Ladd recounts in his memoir of the period, "The Big Bang of consciousness in the late 1960's ignited a tangible sense of wonder and commitment unique in history. And it was against this backdrop, or more accurately because of it, that FM radio was born."[9]

Underground media, principally newspapers, and to a lesser degree the airwaves, served, or believed they served, the constituency experiencing this newfound consciousness. It was a mind-set found both disturbing and troublesome by the nation's leadership. Richard Nixon remarked at the GOP nominating convention in 1968: "They call themselves flower children. I call them spoiled rotten. But a new voice is being heard across America today. It is not the voice of the protesters, the shouters. It is the voice of the Americans who have been forgotten. The non-demonstrators. They're the good people. . . . They're the great silent majority."

PRESAGING THE EMERGENCE

> In the beginning there was AM . . . then along came FM.
>   —John J. O'Connor

FM stereo was commercial underground radio's DNA. It was where experimentation was allowed, because there was so little to lose. Until the mid-1960s, FM moved along in low gear. A nearly negligible listenership provided it with little status and currency among the general public. It was the province of the eggheads and the terminally unhip—the place to tune for Stravinsky and fine arts programming. Most people equated tuning FM to going to a foreign film with subtitles when there was a new action-packed John Wayne movie just around the corner. Most twenty-year-olds had never tuned between 88 and 108 megahertz. Why should they? The cool music and wacky deejays were all over the AM band.

During the first two decades of its existence (1940s–1960s), FM's audience never amounted to more than a fraction of that of its static-ridden, monophonic precursor—AM—and this was to the great chagrin of independent FM operators, in particular. A significant number of FM licenses were held by AM stations, which simulcast their standard broadcast band signals over their FM airwaves. This was done for the sole purpose of economics. Combo licensees (those possessing both an AM and an FM license) saw little reason to originate programming for those scant few who tuned their FM frequencies. It would not be cost efficient, thus they simply duplicated what was on their AM side.

To the Federal Communications Commission, this ultimately constituted a lack of "efficient" use of the band—impeding and inhibiting the medium's ability to grow and flourish. After lengthy urging by unhappy stand-alone FM operators, who felt that combo simulcasting was a primary deterrent to their success, the commission ruled that AM broadcasters in areas of 100,000 or more residents could not simulcast for more than half of their broadcast day. This sent shock waves through the combo operator community, which feared a drain on its profits and resources.

However, this action proved a landmark ruling for FM, finally allowing it to break the shackles that forced it to be little more than an echo chamber Cinderella of its big, bad AM sister. It could now legitimately set out on its own, unimpaired, on a path leading to long-awaited success. Reported the *Wall Street Journal:*

> FM progressive radio began in the mid-1960's when the Federal Communications Commission ruled that companies that owned AM-FM combination stations had to program them separately. Because FM wasn't a money-maker, many stations became a laboratory for new progressive rock music, the antithesis of TOP 40.[10]

Mike Harrison: When the FCC pulled the plug on this cozy situation that combo operators enjoyed, things began to change. Some owners were even open to new and creative ideas to fill the time—ideas that might have cultural and commercial appeal, relevance, and potential. After all, there was little to lose in ratings and revenues.

In FM's bag of tricks was a superior sounding signal, one that was static-free, as well as the ability to broadcast in stereo. The time was right to profit from these attractive features, since the consumer public was becoming increasingly eager to invest in home stereo equipment. Providing a necessary impetus for the marketing of two-channel sound were the recording companies, which were producing more stereophonic records, and not just by classical music artists, as had principally been the case.

> *Scoop Nisker:* This really positioned FM. It was perfect for what would become underground, because it lacked a real commercial audience in the 1960s. Mostly fine arts stuff and beautiful music had been aired. Since it offered stereo, it was inevitable that it would meet up with rock music, which was increasingly being recorded in dual channels.

The eagerness of AM/FM combo broadcasters to cut their potential losses led some to alternative forms of programming, observed Top 40 giant Bruce Morrow:

> What the hell could you put on FM that wouldn't cost an arm and a leg and drain your AM operation? Hey, how about album cuts? . . . Rather than simulate the sound of the Top Forty format, they could stimulate the growing drug culture with the way out music that went along with marijuana and recreational pharmaceuticals. The owners reasoned they could hire strange hippies as FM disc jockeys, letting them play whatever they thought their contemporaries wanted to hear, and, best of all, since they would be on "underground" FM stations, they wouldn't command big salaries like their AM counterparts.[11]

The increasing popularity of rock albums among youth also helped encourage some FMs to abandon their conventional fare and launched them on a quest for disenchanted and disenfranchised radio users—those who had rejected the 45 rpm-driven pop chart radio outlets. By the 1960s, albums, "with their longer songs, more sophisticated musical stylings and challenging themes, had become the choice of the young rock audience that was most passionate about music."[12]

Things were finally happening in the "magic" medium, and this excited many young broadcasters who had begun to lose hope for a more creative and stimulating kind of radio. It was time to bid farewell to the "theater of the mindless."

A different kind of radio for a different kind of time.

Dwight Douglas: We all felt part of an exciting change. Things seemed to be happening on all fronts. In fashion, the Navy pea coat and bell bottom pants appeared. Love beads were worn by both sexes, and hair got longer and longer. Membership in this "club" was not exclusive. Everyone you knew seemed to be joining. The music was the most significant bonding agent. It didn't take long for the orphans of the 1960s to gravitate to the radio orphan—FM. The inspiration was the album cut. The freedom to experience an artist's work the way he or she had put it together was the draw. What AM dictated became irrelevant. AM was the parentally approved medium, and who needed that?

Radio was beginning to relate to young people in a whole new way. Something fresh, titillating, and even a bit threatening was emanating from the radio speaker. Recalls writer Annie Gottlieb:

I heard this song about two A.M.: "Something is happening here/But you don't know what it is/Do you, Mr. Jones?" It was Bob Dylan, and I was listening to the words. And I remember thinking to myself, "What the fuck is this? What is this guy talking about?" It was absolutely hypnotic. It was as if I had just been changed to a different frequency, zapped right into the radio.[13]

SATORI REDUX

Turn On, Tune In, Drop Out.

—Timothy Leary

On the radio format tree, underground has a variety of ancestral, as well as descendant, limbs—family branches. Underground is directly related to what may be most accurately called *freeform* radio, which had its roots in the nocturnal experimentation at fledgling commercial FM stations and in the eclecticism found at some of their commercial-free counterparts in the lower portion of the megahertz band.

From its emergence in the mid-1960s to its deconstruction in the early 1970s, underground radio underwent a variety of personality changes.

Charles Laquidara: Some noncoms were playing at mixing disparate music forms really early on in the 1960s. Then came the underground thing on the commercial side of the street in response to a host of influences in music and society. A little later on, some of these underground outlets were calling themselves alternative, and they were not as loose and unstructured as underground. When the money started being made, a lot of these stations became known as progressive, which had a corporate heart behind its cool exterior. Ultimately, underground and everything that it symbolized was relegated to the scrap heap by album-oriented rock, and playlists and everything else were back. The old music radio principles rejected by the early undergrounders were restored. During this evolution there were other permutations or manifestations of underground that featured their own little spinoffs, like acid and psychedelic rock stations, for example.

[handwritten margin note: decline back to format radio]

Laquidara contends that while underground radio shared qualities and characteristics of the freeform, alternative, and progressive programming approaches (often referred to as one and the same thing), it bore little resemblance to its ultimate successor, album-oriented rock, whose nature and raison d'être were quite different.

The individuals who had a chief role in the development of the commercial underground sound were, not so oddly, radio people to begin with, that is to say, folks who derived their income working the airwaves, many at stations for whose programming they felt little passion.

In discussions focusing on the earliest pioneers of the underground radio phenomenon, dozens of names are bandied about, most commonly Thom O'Hair, Scott Muni, Dave Pierce, Allen Shaw, Mike Harrison, Tom Gamache, Scoop Nisker, Rosco, Ed Bear, Stefan Ponek, Bob McClay, Raechel Donahue, Charles Laquidara, Vaco Cash, Tim Powell, and so on. Some cite early 1960s noncommercial broadcasters like Bob Fass and Larry Yurdin as the preeminent practitioners and innovators of the genre. There are even deejays from 1950s radio who make the list, such as Buck Matthews out of Detroit.

However, the individuals most often placed at the top of the list are Tom Donahue and Larry Miller. Opinions differ as to which of these men should wear the dubious crown "father of underground radio," but Tom Donahue most often gets the nod.

According to trade magazine publisher, radio historian, and former broadcaster Eric Rhoads, Tom Donahue began it all in San Francisco. "He gave birth and nurtured underground into a viable form of radio programming. I don't know anyone else who has as much claim to the title."[14]

Dusty Street: Tom was inspired to create the underground sound when he heard an eleven-minute cut on a Doors album called "The End," in which Jim Morrison says, "Father, I want to kill you. Mother, I want to kill you." Tom said, "I need to be able to play this record on the air." He knew no other station would play anything over a three-minute-and-fifteen-second cut (because "El Paso" by Marty Robbins was the longest single ever). So FM was the only way to go, he figured.

Raechel Donahue: Tom always said everyone else who claimed to have invented underground could be first and he would be happy to be second. He said he was like a South American revolutionary leader taking advantage of an opportunity: "My people are in the streets! I must go out and see which way they are going, for I am their leader!" In my opinion, it was a simultaneous discovery, you know, like when everybody suddenly shows up at school with a yo-yo. Nobody called each other the night before and said to be sure and bring a yo-yo. It just happens. Tom was the first guy to put the thing together with a theory behind it. The aim was to make it as different from Top 40 as possible.

Charles Laquidara: Yeah, Tom really got the thing rolling at KMPX. It wasn't much before then. He knew it was his baby.

Dave Pierce: Well, like Charles, I was back there at the start. Down at the church in Pasadena that housed KPPC. From my perspective, though, Larry Miller really introduced the programming concept that would be more fully developed by Tom Donahue. I think Miller's was the first seed in the underground radio movement, which was watered and cultivated by Donahue and others.

Dave Dixon: Miller was there in front of everyone. He was doing the show that inspired the format. Tom Donahue was a blowhard. His claims are crap! He and his friends were smoking dope and listening to Larry Miller, who brought the sound from Detroit to San Francisco.

Larry Miller: I'm not out to claim any crown. I know Tom Donahue heard my all-night show on KMPX and a few months later the station was doing full-time pretty much what I'd been doing a few hours a night. By then, Tom was programming the station.

SURFACING

Kilo . . . Mother . . . Pot . . . Xray

There are as many stations claiming to have debuted the commercial underground format as there are those claiming to have innovated the sound. Once again, however, two are most frequently cited, and they are KMPX-FM in San Francisco and WOR-FM in New York.

While these two stations are traditionally accorded landmark status, as stated earlier, the coming of the underground format was foreshadowed at other stations as early as the 1950s.

> *Dave Dixon:* I recall, as a kid glued to the radio in Detroit around 1955–1956, a show on WJR-AM. This deejay, Buck Matthews, mixed all kinds of music together in a pretty unrestricted, freeform way, and instead of using the familiar stilted announcer approach of the day, he spoke in a very conversational, laid-back style. He did this on an all-night show, which, I suppose, was considered by management to be the place to try a little something different. Matthews certainly influenced my approach years later in underground/progressive radio. I believe his show on WJR had a significant impact on Larry Miller, too, who was from around Detroit and a young radio fan as well.

Other precursors of FM underground radio could be found on the AM band. For example, Chicago's WCFL-AM offered a freeform mix of rock music around the mid-1960s, featuring groups like the Velvet Underground, Vanilla Fudge, Deep Purple, and the Grateful Dead. Even as the underground sound took up residence on FM, a number of AM outlets (typically of low power), experimented with the "open" technique of music programming. For example, in Newton, Massachusetts, WNTN-AM aired rock album artists in the late 1960s. (See Appendix A.)

A number of early noncommercial stations presaged the arrival of commercial underground radio. Perhaps most significant among them are WBAI-FM and WFMU-FM. At the former, a young deejay named Bob Fass worked the overnight slot, airing a program called "Radio Unnameable." Lynda Crawford wrote of Fass:

Taking the concept of freeform (or birthing it himself?), he began with music, music that no other radio station played, but most important, all kinds of music. He set out to show that all music, be it rock, classical, folk, all music relates to each other and that none of it has to be categorized. . . . The show was completely free, and there you had freeform. Other stations, particularly college stations, began picking up on Bob's show and trying to duplicate it, and then eventually, when it looked as if it might be profitable because of its popularity, commercial radio entered the game. WOR-FM was the first.[15]

Across the river in New Jersey, Larry Yurdin at college station WFMU-FM was doing much the same thing, observed Steve Post. "When the big boys in broadcasting noticed that WBAI and WFMU—of all stations—along with a handful of others around the country were getting respectable FM ratings, they smelled something profitable and invested in the 'youth market.' "[16]

Undoubtedly, stations like those mentioned above helped set the stage for the surfacing of commercial underground radio, which got under way at about the same time on both coasts.

Most radio historians point to WOR-FM in New York as the first commercial outlet to break with the "primary" or single-format approach to music programming. "Beginning in 1966 on New York's WOR-FM, the format known as Progressive or Free Form rejected shouting Top 40 deejays and the formal voices found on adult stations. In their place, progressive enlisted laid-back, conversational communicators who featured album cuts excluded from conventional playlists."[17]

In their retrospective on radio after the arrival of television, media observers Peter Fornatale and Joshua Mills make no bones about which station they believe set the commercial underground radio wheels in motion—WOR-FM. "The evidence clearly shows that Tom Donahue, the so-called 'father of progressive radio,' did not take his first steps until March 1967."[18]

The freeform experiment at WOR lasted only a few short months, and the station was on to other things by the time KMPX-FM in San Francisco introduced Donahue's version of the format in the spring of the following year. New York was not long without a commercial underground station, however. WNEW-FM took up the challenge, at least part-time, in October 1967:

When WOR-FM's non-format was changed in 1967 to the RKO standardized approach instituted by Bill Drake, Muni and some of the station's progressive air personalities and music programmers had to find another home. WNEW-FM took them in and ran with the ball.[19]

During the game of musical chairs on the East Coast, the opposite coast witnessed the launch of its first commercial underground signal at a less than auspicious broadcast outlet in San Francisco.

> *Tim Powell:* KMPX was located at 50 Green Street. It was in a warehouse down by the docks at the northern end of the city. KMPX was the first stereo FM station in California, hence the call letters—K-MultiPleX, not KiloMotherPotXray that some underground jocks claimed later. It was a foreign language brokered station before its conversion to underground. This means that there were Chinese hours, with announcers in Chinese who usually bought the time in bulk packages from KMPX and then sold airtime with the difference between the fee paid the station and the advertising revenue being the profit.

A few months after assuming the programming reins at KMPX-FM, Tom Donahue took on its sister station, KPPC-FM in Southern California, simultaneously working his magic at both. The underground radio programming genre, the "nonformat" format, was beginning to make a sound that was being heard not only at both ends of the country but in between as well.

In 1968 dozens of stations around the United States were offering listeners their own brand of underground radio. Most large metropolitan areas boasted what many were calling "flower power" stations, including cities like Detroit, Cleveland, Chicago, and St. Louis. This was no longer an avante garde form of radio restricted to the urban enclaves of the East and West.

> Freaks established and tuned into a few hip FM stereo stations. KMPX and KSAN in the Bay Area, WBAI or "Radio Unnameable" in New York, and "Up Against the Wall FM" in Madison were some of the first, and soon other listener-sponsored stations went on the air in many other cities, including Los Angeles, Houston, and Washington, D.C. All playing the music and all giving clues to the counterculture.[20]

This same year also saw the entire staff of KMPX, led by Tom Donahue, migrate to KSAN-FM. The action came after a months-long strike against the management of KMPX after it removed Donahue from his duties at KPPC, arguing that he was spreading himself too thin and neglecting some of his duties. The irony of the phrase "spreading himself too thin" did not escape the attention of many, given Donahue's prodigious size.

At this early stage in underground radio's evolution, two stations were frequently held up as models of the genre—KSAN and WNEW. Both were doing reasonably well attracting listeners and advertisers. While often compared, the stations had forged their own distinct personas. In her thorough organizational analysis of KSAN, *Hip Capitalism*, Susan Krieger notes that WNEW's program director perceived a difference in the way the two stations went about designing their programming.

> He felt their approaches were different in that Donahue had introduced his change on KMPX in opposition to abuses of Top 40 radio, he had been idealistic about it, while on WNEW-FM, they were more technical and analytic in their thinking. They thought about changing the format in terms of what would make good radio and good business sense. Their thinking was that album cuts had an intellectual appeal, and that the programming should be compatible with the style of music.[21]

Scott Muni: You know, I think we were all fairly individual in our sounds, and that really had most to do with the available talent in an area. Each station drew on their local talent and so had a pretty distinctive flavor. Every on-air person had a specialty, it seemed. When stations took the challenge to convert their FMs, available talent ended up on the air, and sometimes that resulted in a lot of creativity. In the end, though, I think there was a collective flow of genius juice that everyone contributed to in their own unique way.

John Gorman: We all attempted to do our own thing, although the format had been discovered on both coasts before it made its way to Cleveland, and when something is already out there, there's bound to be some mirroring.

Shelley Grafman: Of course, that makes sense. But the issues and events occurring within a given station's signal area, as well as the lifestyles indigenous to it, inevitably influence a station's sound. This was true at KSHE in St. Louis, like every place else—New York, San Francisco. You name it.

Charles Laquidara: Yeah, that's right. WBCN very much was Boston. Because of this, it had a more folksy flavor. The station reflected the community, its mood and makeup. This city is different than any other, and the station reflected that difference in what it did on the air.

Carla Brooks Johnston: While much of the experimenting was with music, political change was also on the air. By 1968, a group of us interested in turning local city government around found a friend in Tony Cennamo, a disc jockey on local Boston station WCAS. Between his musical selections, he let us call in, or be guests on the show to discuss the total disregard of local government for kids who had to play in barren glass-littered lots and go to schools without hot water or toilet paper. Tony was so successful that WCAS management fired him and shifted to a nostalgic music format. We were so successful that we elected an Episcopal cleric mayor, got the *Boston Globe* to do its Pulitzer Prize winning "Spotlight" Series that resulted in indictments of several former mayors. I became Mayor's Coordinator of Federal Funds, got a HUD grant, and hired Tony.

By late 1968, there were over five dozen commercial underground radio stations in operation around the country. The following summer, San Francisco alone could claim a half dozen, while New York could boast only half that figure. One company (Metromedia) owned the stations that *Billboard* magazine ranked as the two top underground stations in the country—KSAN and WNEW.

ILLUMINATING THE UNDERGROUND

It was a happening that happened.

—Abbie Hoffman

There are those who view underground radio as a natural outgrowth of the ongoing development of the sixties generation counterculture. "Some 50,000 people took classes at free universities annually, while daily a larger number of young Bostonians read the *RealPaper* or listened to the underground message on WBCN," observed social historian Terry H. Anderson.[22]

From the perspectives of those who were participants in underground's launch, there were a multitude of contributing factors which gave buoyancy to commercial radio's only ever freeform programming genre.

Dave Pierce: It was evolutionary for certain. At some point rock was coming to FM radio. That it happened in 1967–1968, exploding by 1969, coincides with the height of the revolution. The near anarchy in the streets spilled into the new FM rockers' managerial structure and opened the gates for the creative flow. But it was still commercial radio. Broadcasters, even with long hair, were doing it for the dollars. The bonus was the fun and excitement and the joy of being the first (and sadly only) to do it right.

Russ Gibb: We called the underground the people who were beginning to protest the war in Vietnam, those expressing concerns about the environment, and those kids who were using marijuana. So the atmosphere was forming for a brand of counter Top 40 radio. So when I was asked about what to do with the FM, I suggested doing everything the opposite of AM. Instead of talking fast, we should talk slowly, long pauses, and let's play long album cuts. We launched the sound on a Sunday, and young people started responding. I was known as "Uncle Russ" on the air, and I ran the Grandy Ballroom. Tiny Tim worked for me. Tim was before the trends. Hip before hip. Things were wild and loose. We kind of did our thing. I was the deejay who began the Paul McCartney is dead rumor, and the audience responded in an almost hysterical way.

Larry Miller: Responsive to our listeners was what we were. I'd say the most immediate consideration for the creation of underground radio was the obvious need for stations that would play the music that people were listening to at home and the way they were listening to it. We had grown up with rock and roll as teen music in the 1950s. By the mid-1960s, the Beatles and Dylan had led the way in creating a new rock genre that was for young adults in their twenties. They made it okay for grown-ups to listen to rock. We had begun listening to whole albums, not just singles. The theme album, such as "Sgt. Pepper," hadn't really been developed, but albums like "Rubber Soul" and "Revolver" or Dylan's "Bringing It All Back Home" were obviously more than just a collection of singles. Top 40 had become unlistenable to us. There was too much teen orientation, jingles, moronic deejays, stupid teenybopper songs. There definitely was a strongly perceived need for adult album rock radio.

Thom O'Hair: Like Richard Nixon used to say, "Let's go to the map." First off, the only underground/progressive stations were all commercial. That's all there was in those days. I consider May 21, 1967, as ground zero for underground radio. It was with Tom Donahue and friends at

KMPX. Before that, there were fragments of the soon to be whole out there. For example, Stefan Ponek had the "Sunshine Hour" on KSAN. It was a half-hour-long folk music–based program. Bits and pieces of what would become underground radio were being aired at college stations around the country, but Tom Donahue birthed the child on that May day, which began the trip. Why it happened? Who can really say for sure. Tom would talk of sitting around home as a deejay and playing music and realizing that the music that he was playing for himself and his friends was not the same music he was playing for a living on the air. I always thought this was a good observation. Donahue and I would talk about how playing music for each other was a passion. Everyone in radio did it. It was the height of radio coolness to have the gear in your home to mix music. This was long before any consumer equipment was available to handle these chores.

Frank Wood: In 1967, I aired this real eclectic freeform mix of music on a program I called the "Jelly Pudding Hour." It was Cincinnati's first exposure to this kind of radio. We became the area's spokesperson for the counterculture generation, and I bet I knew our entire cume by their first name.

Stefan Ponek: It was a fertile time for program ideas. I had this bright idea at KSFR (later to be called KSAN) in 1967 to expand on the station's "lively arts" format. My plan was to include recognition of the new and original rock music out there, which I listened to endlessly on KMPX, where Tom Donahue and his air people were sounding loaded on the air and very much in touch with the music and Haight Ashbury scene, as it was. Metromedia's general manager, Reid Leath, a reclusive southern good ol' boy type reminiscent of Arthur Carlson on "WKRP," because he would hide in his office with a copy of *Field and Stream* and had no idea what to do with the radio station, allowed me an hour on Saturday nights to experiment with my idea, which I called "Underground Sunshine." This moniker was later to be expropriated by Donahue for use on the LA station that he got control of, but I'm getting ahead of myself. Within a couple weeks of my experiment, which included tracking the Electric Prune's "Mass" and a collage of other stony stuff, the KMPX crew was on the street striking against the station's owner, Leon Crosby. In subsequent shows, it was my good fortune to bring in several of the KMPXers as guest deejays to provide them a venue to espouse their cause. It, too, brought commercials to KSFR. That got attention. The show went to four hours. Money does talk. What followed is not very well known. Having my way with Metromedia's local manager, Leath, I began to convince him to change the format to the kind of thing KMPX had been doing. It didn't look like that group would ever resolve their differences anyway, so there was an opening, and I really wanted to be a part of that staff. KSFR was a union station, paying far better than KMPX ever could, so that was obviously an attraction. Anyway, Leath was going for it, but there were questions. What if their success as a band of hippies emboldened them further and they were uncontrollable later on? Metromedia could not afford the kind of public disapproval being heaped upon poor little Crosby. After some contact with the company's higher-ups in New York, Leath unleashed me to quietly contact each KMPX deejay to see if they would come to KSFR. I was to get Bear, Postle, McClay. Then gradually we could pick and choose our new team. So then, the idea was to have the format and control, which would disarm Donahue, who was perceived as a potentially dangerous person. Whether he would be a part of the plan was initially left unanswered. We wanted to see how things would unfold. How it did unfold was that Donahue hopped on a plane to New York as soon as he got wind of how I was talking to Bear and Postle. There he pitched the idea to Leath's bosses of his assuming programming duties at KSFR, keeping me as part of the bargain. Interestingly, while I felt outmaneuvered and overpowered, it didn't bother me that much, because I got what I really wanted, which was to be a part of that hip KMPX group. So KSFR would quickly become KSAN, the country's flagship underground station.

Dan Carlisle: A lot of us who ended up in underground were kind of marking time for it to happen. Most of the FM pioneers of the so-called underground radio format were the children of mid-fifties rock radio. The presentation they heard was more freewheeling than the "Drake" format-dominated 1960s. We grew up listening to performers who certainly played the hits but, most importantly, they made the hits. If a deejay loved and was moved by a song, you may have heard it two or three times in a row. In addition, his on-air persona often eclipsed the station itself. Deejays were the reason we tuned in. We also had a sense that they loved the same music we did. I began my commercial radio career doing the strict playlist thing. Talk was very limited to specifics. While this was excellent training in the basics of broadcasting, many of us felt that the free-wheeling style of the 1950s was more fun and better radio.

Lee Abrams: God knows, things were tight at the pop chart outlets back then. Underground was a reaction to that and the growing popularity of a new generation of bands and sounds, which were too radical for the hit-single Top 40–driven stations. Guys like Hendrix needed their own format where their music could be exposed and thrive. Top 40 was prepared to only play the short version of an album hit and then only after dark, sandwiched between "Mony Mony" and "Strangers in the Night." Underground was also a reaction to the changing cultural climate. It was a vehicle for the new gestalt that was emerging in the air and on the street.

Roland Jacopetti: It sure was that, I'd have to agree. I listened to Tom Donahue back when he was jocking on KYA and also to Sly Stone in his teenage deejay days, and even without a clear knowledge that most of radio was formatted and that the deejays were pretty strictly regulated, it was obvious to me that what these people were doing was much more exciting than current Top 40. For me, the inspiration behind the emergence of underground radio was in the desire on the part of radio people and music people to share their delight in what they knew and loved with the public.

Ed Shane: At the time, I think we all felt we had something unique to convey. The music, the culture, the counterculture, the hippie movement all nudged us on. All of these things did contribute, and looking back they seem to me to be in unique alignment with other forces of the time that really helped establish the milieu for the emergence of commercial underground radio. I see these as:

   1. Demographics—The baby boom (as it came to be called) inflated high school and college enrollments. The first group of the post–World War II children were in their teens, gathering in a social environment that had not been witnessed since the Great Depression—similarities of experience and similarities of interest.

Unlike the Depression, however, there was no suffering. If anything, the baby boomers were experiencing the greatest period of affluence in American history. The road structure was linking our cities; automobiles were affordable. As backdrop to the social interaction, there was music this group could call its own.

2. Technology—Often overlooked as a contributing factor was the ability of pop music groups to amplify themselves and their music. This was a galvanizing force for kids who had discovered their own music on Top 40 radio, which played the two-and-a-half-minute cuts, but in live performances there was more. That is, more music in longer versions and more elaborate instrumentation, and, of course, more volume.

Another technological factor was the long-playing record. Once the sole province of the classical music lover or jazz buff, the LP allowed baby boom teenagers to collect all their favorite forty-fives on one disc, instead of ten or twelve separate seven-inch records. Once they got used to playing 33 1/3 rpm records, instead of forty-fives, they saw the parallel between the LP and the live performance.

One last note on technology. Commercial underground radio could not have happened without FM. Enhanced audio transmission paralleled the LP and the more elaborate instrumentation. In addition, there were FM signals in most large markets that were either unused or underutilized. The risk seemed low for broadcasters who didn't know what to do with their facilities. Creative energies demanded experimentation. What a surprise that large companies provided the platform.

3. Politics—The concern for the war in Vietnam was just building in the mid-1960s. Overshadowing even Vietnam were the dreams shattered by the death of John Kennedy. The baby boom children identified with him, even if they knew nothing of him or his politics. (You might even say *especially* if they knew nothing of him or his politics.)

He seemed young, accessible, and with a fascinating family that was constantly pictured on the new TV sets that America was acquiring at an astonishing rate. Kennedy was an icon for the new, emerging generation.

Kennedy's assassination created, among other things, skepticism. The escalation of the Vietnam War just a few years later fed that skepticism and turned into cynicism among some young Americans. The years that followed—the Johnson administration, the Nixon and Watergate years—further undermined politics as a high-minded activity.

Note that in none of this have I mentioned the drug culture. Sure, it contributed, because it altered (some say "enhanced") attitudes toward any of the aligned forces I've cited. I feel that drugs were a secondary force, not primary.

Al Wilson: Look, it all had to do with cultural transformation. There was this massive continental drift occurring on about every front you can imagine. The format was symbolic of that change.

Tim Powell: There are several problems when attempting to explain the forces that created underground commercial radio—a crappy term. One is making it understandable, especially to those born after JFK's assassination, what a brainwashed country this one was. Second, there were sociological, technological, and musicial changes which contributed to the art form. That these coincided at a point when radio was in a stasis rather points to the reasons for its inception.

Mike Harrison: When all is said and done, bottom line considerations always carry plenty of weight. There was an emerging pop culture industry to serve the growing anti-establishment tastes and needs. Everything from head shops to alternative clothing stores, nightclubs, boutiques, newpapers and magazines, movies, concerts, and a lot more, sprung up, and this industry needed a place to advertise.

THE ERSATZ UNDERGROUND

Underground, my ass!

—Eldridge Cleaver

Not everyone felt comfortable with the designation "underground" for this new brand of radio. It mystified some and embarrassed others. It was too weighty for more than a few broadcasters and media critics. The term "underground," with its clandestine and subversive connotations, was wholly inappropriate, thought Black Panther leader Eldridge Cleaver, who scoffed at the notion that stations that could readily be tuned on any receiver from the White House to Shaker Heights could be a part of the legitimate or actual underground movement.

Cleaver's view was shared by some within the broadcast industry, including some who worked the new programming sound.

> *Ed Shane:* Underground was an unfortunate misnomer, because the stations operated on licensed frequencies owned by some of America's largest broadcast groups. Looking back at it from the perspective of the late 1990s, what irony! However, I recall writing in my station's (WPLO) programming policy statement at the time the following:
>
>> Because we are so label-conscious these days, the label "underground" has stuck to radio stations that could NEVER be underground, owing to their control by the FCC. Actually, "underground" is a strictly political term that connotes a never-seen network of spies and counter-spies, who might command guerilla attacks. True underground stations pop up during times of political unrest, and they are TRUE undergrounds. They broadcast propaganda until they are discovered by their enemies and destroyed. So the term "underground," as applied to this kind of radio, is really inaccurate and inappropriate. I prefer "contemporary attitude" radio.

Tom Donahue himself was not a proponent of the term, but he also felt that labels such as progressive, freeform, and alternative were not much better. He may well have preferred Shane's term.

> *Raechel Donahue:* Tom wasn't all that interested in labeling things, but he would probably have agreed that the format had something to do with contemporary attitudes about music and culture.

The perspective among many mainstream broadcasters and media observers was that the format had a lot less to do with political ideals than it did with the fact that its practitioners were a bunch of social misfits and industry rejects. "They were a whole different breed. Lots of these guys were like college kids who had to start their own fraternities because none of the mainstream frats would have them," observed Bruce Morrow.[23]

> *Tim Powell:* The people who were in FM when this new thing happened were, at least to a degree, a bunch of lameheads. There was a lot of everything motivating people and some of it pretty inexplicable.

FREEDOM:

KSFX
103.7
SAN FRANCISCO

Freedom of expression was what it was about.

> *Robert Hilliard:* Again, I think it is important to make the
> distinction between the commercial underground outlets
> and those not licensed to sell commercials. One might argue
> that true underground radio existed in the form of illegal
> stations, the likes of which were later devised by people such
> as electronics genius Lorenzo Milam. He drove the feds nuts
> with his clandestine signals that broadcast anti-government
> messages on a wide variety of topics.

A substantial number of social and political historians and analysts
suggests that the themes embraced by the counterculture protesters in the
streets were not consistently reflected in the day-to-day banter of these
self-styled underground radio stations, whose raison d'être, they contend,
had more to do with album rock and flower power than with the long, hard
march toward social and cultural transformation and reform. To David
Caute, underground media were nothing more than a reaction, a "Yippie
remedy"[24] to the activity occurring beyond their sound proof walls. If the
radio undergrounders were leftist at all it was because they loved "nothing
more than to issue calls to arms for causes that have already been won,"
wrote Suzanne Labin in *Hippies, Drugs and Promiscuity*.[25]

LOVE IS IN THE AIR

To ape the magnanimity of love.

—George Meredith

In 1968, ABC-FM Radio felt it knew what the revolution was all about.
To the network, it was conveyed in one four letter word—love! In what
follows, Allen Shaw describes what led him to the concept of a nationwide
spin-off (some felt rip-off) of the underground programming genre and how
it was ultimately launched and executed.

> *Allen Shaw:* For me the long strange trip into underground
> radio began in the fall of 1965. I was twenty-two years old,
> just out of college, and working the 7 to 11 P.M. shift as a
> Top 40 deejay at WPTR-AM in Albany, New York. I was
> supposed to be playing the top-selling hits of the day, such
> as "Everybody Loves a Clown" by Gary Lewis and the
> Playboys and "Lover's Concerto" by the Toys. I found
> myself slipping in unapproved cuts off the Rolling Stones,
> Beatles, and Bob Dylan albums. This was, of course, break-
> ing the format rules of the station, a clear act of revolution-

ary protest. It was motivated by boredom with the narrow and predictable pop rock lyrics and music that stood essentially unchanged for a decade since rock and roll began with Little Richard, Fats Domino, and Elvis Presley. I was giving in to an irresistible impulse to go beyond playing the records with the big holes (forty-fives) to the new frontier of playing the big records with the little holes (LPs). I felt that some of the secondary cuts off many of the albums in release during this time were as good or better than the record company's designated "single." Dick Lawrence, the program director, finally caught on to what I was doing and told me, in no uncertain terms, that the public would decide through their purchase of single records what we would play. Not me! This was a lesson that, in later years, would prove valuable to me.

A year later, while employed as assistant program director at Chicago Top 40 station WCFL, I began listening at home to promotional copies of the new rock albums by bands unfamiliar to me, like Vanilla Fudge, Jimi Hendrix, and the Velvet Underground. I found these new sounds very interesting and exciting. They were clearly a radical departure from the happy and breezy 1960s sounds of the Turtles' "Happy Together" and the Association's "Windy," which were the staple of the music we were playing on the station at the time.

Several new albums released during the summer and fall of 1967 had a major impact on me. The Rolling Stones' "Satanic Majesty's Request," the Beatles' "Magical Mystery Tour," the Doors, and Procol Harum blew me away. They were so innovative, so uncomfortable, so compelling that they couldn't be ignored. These new sounds should be on the air, I reasoned, but where and how? The uniqueness of the sound, a total departure, really, was problem number one. How could we mix these long strange cuts in with Paul Revere and the Raiders and Leslie Gore?

I asked WCFL's PD and general manager, Ken Draper, if we could get some of this new album product on the air. Draper couldn't reconcile the length of the cuts and differences in sound with the singles on the station's playlist either. However, he did agree to give me one hour between 8 and 9 P.M. on Sunday nights to expose this new rock product. I was thrilled! I asked Ron Britain, the most intelligent, creative, and unconventional personality on the station, to host the show. We called it "Ron Britain's

Subterranean Circus." Underground radio had come to Chicago, even if for only an hour a week and in mono- phonic sound.

It was during 1967 that two other events furthered my interest in progressive rock and underground radio. The first was my attendance at the Bill Gavin Radio Programming Conference in Las Vegas. I attended a panel discussion of new trends in radio. On that panel was this large, long- haired, bearded man with a deep voice, who spoke passionately about what he was doing in San Francisco on FM station KMPX. This was Tom Donahue. He described the station as a place where deejays played an eclectic mix of blues, folk, and progressive rock without any restrictions on the playlist. There were no jingles or structure, just total freedom of expression. I walked away from that panel inspired by his words. There, indeed, was something going on in music, formats, and FM, something that was definitely going to change things as we had known them.

The second event occurred in late 1967. Lou Reed and the Velvet Underground were opening for Jimi Hendrix at Aaron Russo's Kinetic Playground in Chicago (Russo had opened the trendy psychedelic club, the Electric Circus, in New York). I had gotten WCFL promotionally tied into the Playground and was backstage talking to Lou Reed while Hendrix was playing. Despite the Velvet Underground's druggy, hipper than hip image, I found Reed to be a very intelligent, middle-class kid, capable of carrying on a very normal conversation. So I took the opportunity to ask him how widespread he thought the public's interest in pro- gressive rock music was and if he thought it had potential for being a full-time radio format on an FM station. He told me about WOR-FM's brief experiment with progressive rock in New York and how much response it got from people in the city and how WNEW-FM was doing a similar format with great results. Reed pointed out that the num- ber of new rock bands with albums was increasing rapidly and that the record companies felt that this, in fact, was going to be the next big event in pop music. He assured me that I'd be certain to succeed if I put this music on FM full-time.

Looking back on that night, I realize how oblivious I was to the future historical importance of Jimi Hendrix and Lou Reed. If I had known, I would have taped my conversation with Reed and would have been in the audience watching and listening to Hendrix. What I did know that night was that I would do whatever it took to put progressive rock on an FM station somewhere.

The following Monday I sat down with George Yahraes, a former fellow Northwestern University campus radio station (WNUR) staffer. George was now promotion director at WCFL, and he shared my enthusiasm for progressive music, feeling, too, that it possessed the potential to be a new radio format. George and I worked long hours at night and on weekends preparing sample music tapes and graphics for what we decided to call the "LOVE" concept.

Our idea was an admittedly slick commercial approach to treating the new rock music and cultural events that were emerging at the time. Being an eternal idealist and a middle-class Catholic boy, I thought the "underground" should be brought above ground and into the light of day and [that] all the negatives of the counterculture—the drugs, the anti-establishment political rhetoric, the anti-Amerika attitude—could be downplayed in favor of the positives—the great new music, freedom of expression, brotherhood, and LOVE.

I thought the music, album rock, played in stereo high fidelity on FM, was really the single most important and long-lasting aspect of what was happening. I had difficulty with the undisciplined, rambling, and often boring product of the so-called freeform, underground stations that had begun to spring up across the country.

After George and I put the concept together and prepared a flip-chart presentation which showed the events of the youth culture that were signaling a new market for a different kind of format for radio, I called virtually every FM station owner in Chicago. I discovered that most of these stations were put on the air by broadcast engineers, who viewed these frequencies as technical toys or hobbies. Their ideas on programming were very pure and unaggressive. From their perspective, only classical, easy listening, or jazz were appropriate forms of music to be aired on FM. Nasty rock music on FM was clearly an undesirable thing for them.

Frustrated by my total strikeout with Chicago FM station owners, in desperation I called the larger network and group-owned FM station operators. I called the heads of Westinghouse, CBS, NBC, and ABC in New York. All but CBS agreed to meet with George and me to hear our presen-

tation. CBS was happy with their "Young Sound," an automated instrumental format, featuring orchestral covers of
contemporary songs.

We made our first presentation to Steve Lubunski and
Steve Riddleberger at NBC. They seemed intrigued, but
asked if we thought the concept would work on NBC's AM
stations, which were flourishing at the time. We thought
not. Westinghouse was not sure how many FM stations they
actually owned. They had been giving their FM stations
away or shutting them down to save on power bills as they
saw little commercial future for them.

The reception at ABC Radio was quite different. We met
with Ralph Beaudin, radio division vice president, and Hal
Neal, [ABC-]owned radio station president. Ralph had
recently come to ABC from the general managership of
the legendary WLS-AM in Chicago and had just launched
the highly innovative, demographically targeted four radio networks for ABC. Hal Neal had made his mark in the
early 1960s as the general manager of WABC-AM in New
York, helping put it into radio history as America's most
popular Top 40 station. These guys were clearly not afraid
of innovation or of rock and roll music. They presided over
the most successful group of AM stations in the country:
WABC, New York; KQV, Pittsburgh; WXYZ, Detroit; WLS, Chicago; KABC, Los Angeles; and KGO, San Francisco.

George Yahraes and I went through our flip-card presentation, which documented the percentage of albums that
were progressive rock (23 percent of the top 100) and were
not being played on the air. We made our point about
people listening to these albums on high fidelity stereo
record players at home and how they should want to hear
them on high fidelity stereo FM radio stations, if they were
available. We described the cultural changes taking
place among the youth of America that would lead them
to seek a different presentation of rock music than that
which was being done on AM Top 40 radio. We described
the "LOVE" concept, taking only the positives from the
counterculture movement.

After we finished our pitch, Ralph Beaudin, who, I was
later to learn, had an abrupt aspect to his personality that
was not to be taken seriously, got up from his seat and said,
"Well, I've got a train to catch." How's that for a cold
reaction? Our hearts sank. Obviously we had struck out.
While Hal Neal attempted to console us, his phone rang. It

was Ralph calling from his office to suggest that George and I come to the ABC Radio managers' meeting in Puerto Rico next month to present our ideas to the station general managers. We were elated!

Our presentation to the ABC station managers in Puerto Rico, in February of 1968, was well received. The only problem was money. Despite ABC Radio's resources, ABC-TV was still trailing CBS and NBC, and it needed to spend millions on its long-overdue conversion to color. A proposed merger between ITT and ABC had just fallen apart, so ABC did not have the ready capital to invest in the development of FM radio at the moment. Nonetheless, I kept pressing ABC to go forward with the FM project throughout the spring of 1968. Hal Neal asked me if we could do it very inexpensively on an automated basis on all seven FM outlets. George and I worked up a budget calling for less than $300,000 to program all of the ABC owned FM stations, with tapes produced in New York and mailed to the stations each week. We proposed having a single personality on the air all the time. Finally, Hal and Ralph decided to go forward with the project. George and I were hired to report to work in June of 1968. My title was director of FM special projects.

As I was driving from Chicago to New York that June to report to my new job at the network, I heard on the radio that Robert Kennedy had been assassinated in Los Angeles. This was the start of a bad summer for America, especially for the U.S. soldiers in Vietnam and the antiwar protesters, who met the heavy hand of Chicago's Mayor Richard J. Daley during the Democratic National Convention.

Once at ABC in New York, George and I began to lay out the logistics required to get "LOVE" on the air. I was not prepared for all of the administrative obstacles, such as getting the engineers' union and the announcers' union to modify their rules and pay scales to accommodate what was to become the first long-form radio program syndication ever attempted. One major piece of the puzzle not yet found was the on-air talent who would become the round the clock host of "LOVE."

While visiting my wife and two-year-old son in Chicago, who had not yet joined me in New York, I happened to punch in WLS-AM on a Sunday evening to hear a deep, commanding voice coming out of the speaker. "This is

Silhouette, and I'm John Rydgren." Next came the Byrds singing "The Times They Are a Changing." I was fascinated by the curious contrast between this apparent voice from heaven and rock music in the same program. I knew I had found the voice for "LOVE." Calling WLS the next day, I found out that the program was produced by the Radio/TV Department of the American Lutheran Church in Minneapolis. I called the offices of the church and asked for John Rydgren. I told him of our "LOVE" project for ABC-FM and asked if he would have an interest in being our full-time host. He said he would be willing to meet with me and discuss it further. We met in New York a couple of weeks later and reached an agreement.

John was actually an ordained minister of the Lutheran Church. He had a secular view of his ministry and felt that what we were planning with "LOVE" was consistent with his personal and religious views. With the obvious religious connotation, we settled on "Brother John" for his on-air name.

The concept of "LOVE" was to play the best cuts off the most popular new progressive rock albums with Brother John doing preproduced vignettes in between each cut. John wrote these himself. They dealt with the Vietnam War, racism, drug abuse, life's meaning, the music, and, of course, love. I also hired Howard Smith, columnist for the *Village Voice*, to do interviews with the musicians, actors, writers, and others who were part of the new culture. Howard's features ran hourly and were titled "Scenes," also the name of his newspaper column. Between 1969 and 1970, Howard interviewed John and Yoko, Andy Warhol, Jim Morrison, Bill Graham, Jimi Hendrix, and many others. We also set up telephone recorders in every market where listeners could call in and make a statement or tell a story. We would edit these into features to run once per hour. It was called "The American Dialogue Line."

Most of the FM stations owned by ABC already had some form of automation equipment in place. For those that didn't, we had it installed. Most of the stations were pressed into giving up the simulcast of the AM sister station's programming when the FCC forced them to do separate programming a couple of years earlier. The ABC-FM stations were airing everything from Broadway show tunes to easy listening and classical music.

On February 28, 1969, we in the ABC-FM Special Projects Group were finally ready to launch the "LOVE" concept. We recorded twenty-five hours of programming per week in New York and high-speed duplicated these tapes for each of the seven ABC-owned FM outlets. Our syndication manager, T. J. Johnson, was kept busy getting the tapes recorded, duplicated, and mailed each week.

The initial reaction of the establishment press and radio listeners to "LOVE" was favorable. The weekly listenership of the ABC-owned FM stations jumped 750,000 per week to 1,500,000 in the first six months. The underground press, however, panned us as "overly slick," "corporate rock," and "the network giant ripping off the counterculture." We were undaunted.

I was never unclear of the fact that whatever we did had to be financially successful. ABC was not in the business of providing nonprofit programming for the benefit of any culture. We were ABC, not the BBC. Soon we were getting inquiries from other independent FM station owners in smaller markets as to the availability of "LOVE" programming for their stations. We decided to sell the product to others and eventually syndicated it to stations in Illinois, Texas, Michigan, California, Pennsylvania, and Ohio.

I thought it would be cool to have some progressive rock station ID jingles produced for all the stations carrying "LOVE." We had been using a jingle ID series I had produced with PAMS in Dallas, but they sounded too much like the jingles PAMS had been producing successfully for years for WABC-AM and hundreds of other Top 40 stations around the country. ABC had a director of music, Harry Sosnick. He suggested we record the ID series in England in order to get a British sound as well as avoid the cost of residual payments to American union musicians. Harry hired Clay Pitts, a rock-based composer working in New York. George Yahraes, Harry Sosnick, Clay Pitts, and myself collaborated on writing the music and lyrics for the jingle ID series, and then we flew to London to record them at Marble Arch Studio.

We needed a lead male vocalist to do the entire session. Harry had arranged for a half dozen struggling British rock singers to audition. One kid stood out immediately with his unique vocal sound and raw talent. We hired him for about 200 pounds to work with us the whole week. After the recording sessions, we would buy the young singer dinner.

He often brought his lyricist with him and talked about the desire to get a record contract with an American record label. He gave me a demo disc that he had recorded. The disc contained about a dozen songs that he and his lyricist had composed. It was quite good, and I told him we would play some of these songs on the "LOVE" tapes and that I would pass the disc on to Jay Lasker, president of ABC Records, which I did.

A few months later, the New York promoter for MCA Records walked into my office and gave me what he described as a "great new album from a new artist they had just signed in England." I said, "Hey, this is the kid we hired to sing on our station ID jingles last fall in London." I was looking at the first Elton John/Bernie Taupin album released in the United States.

Elton John and ABC-FM became linked for the next decade. Elton agreed to do our first live radio rock concert on WABC-FM on November 17, 1970. It was released as an album titled "11/17/70." His widely popular, mainstream rock music proved to be a definitive and valuable staple of the kind of music our FM stations were going to play throughout the 1970s.

By the summer of 1970, we were reaching a crossroads at ABC-FM. It had become obvious that FM listening was growing nationally. It was also clear that Metromedia and other independent FM stations that featured live deejays and a more politically active, freeform approach to progressive rock radio were getting higher ratings than our centrally produced and automated "LOVE" format. We had already begun to add more live on-air talent to each station. We recruited Dave Herman from WMMR in Philadelphia and Bob Lewis (Bobaloo) from WABC-AM to do live shifts on the FM side. We added twenty-five more hours to the "LOVE" tapes each week with Jimmy Rabbitt and Murray Roman hosting these additional hours. We also had begun to take a more aggressive political position against the war and the Nixon administration. But that was not enough.

There also were administrative and sales problems for the ABC-FM stations, due to the fact that the general managers of the stations were also running the AM stations in each market. FM was considered by many of the AM managers to be at best a joke, and at worst an embarrassment. There was also the identity confusion caused by the FM stations still sharing the same call letters as their AM counterparts in each market.

Hal Neal called me to his office one day in the summer and said, "Allen, I believe, and I know you believe, that if the FM stations are going to grow beyond this point, we are going to have to separate them from AM. We need to set up a separate-owned FM station division, and I want you to run it." I was happy with the concept but surprised that he wanted me to run it. I was twenty-six years old. I thought of myself as a programmer. I had never been in sales. I didn't know much about budgets or management, so I asked him why it wouldn't make more sense to hire someone with sales and management experience from the AM station group to run the FM division. I would be content to continue on in my role as group program director. Hal's typical cut-to-the-bottom-line response was, "You're right about your lack of experience, but you are the only one who believes that FM can ever beat AM. That's your most important qualification. You'll learn the rest the hard way."

I swallowed hard and realized that Hal was giving me his vote of confidence and an opportunity of a lifetime. Against my gut feeling, I agreed to take on the challenge.

ABC was now in the financial position to make a significant investment in its FM radio stations. I was authorized to hire a general manager and program director for each of the stations. We had to come up with new call letters for each station, too. This resulted in WRIF for Detroit, WDVE for Pittsburgh, WDAI for Chicago, KAUM for Houston, and KSFX for San Francisco. A salesperson came up with KLOS for Los Angeles. Dave Herman and I, while discussing new call letters for New York, happened to notice a new Frank Zappa album sitting on my desk. One of the cuts was Zappa's cover of the old Four Deuces R&B classic, "W.P.L.J." ("White Port and Lemon Juice . . . it sure taste good to me"). They had to be the new call letters for WABC-FM, and so they were.

I had become convinced, with the Vietnam War and anti-Nixon protests reaching a peak and the amazing Woodstock event, that we should not only go live in all of our markets, but we should also join the more successful Metromedia and other vanguard FM rock stations around the country, such as WBCN in Boston, WABX in Detroit, and WEBN in Cincinnati, and do full freeform, socially and politically active radio. We were going to become totally involved in, and a reflection of, the American counterculture. This meant that "LOVE" and Brother John would have to go. It was a tough decision for me personally, but I felt it was the right one. John understood the situation and moved to Los Angeles as a personality on KRTH-FM.

I explained the shift in direction to Hal Neal, and to my surprise he did not disagree. He discussed the change with Elton Rule, who had just become president of the broadcast division of ABC, which included all television and radio operations. ABC Chairman Leonard Goldenson was also asked for his blessing. The only restrictions put on us were that there be no obscenities or promotion of illegal drugs. There was not a word about political commentary from my corporate supervisors.

Having been given all the freedom and money we needed, in the fall of 1970, I went about the task of hiring all the highest profile and most radical underground radio personnel available. One of my first hires was Larry Yurdin. Larry had just organized a highly publicized and praised Alternative Media Conference at Goddard College. He overflowed with ideas and enthusiasm for what he called "alternative radio." His energy and passion for doing idealized freeform, socially and politically conscious and active radio was contagious. He also was connected with most of the underground FM radio station people around the country. Hiring Larry to work with me on a group basis gave the ABC-FM radio stations instant counterculture credibility, plus immediate access to on-air talent and programming personnel for the many positions we had to fill.

During the winter of 1971, all seven of the ABC-owned FM stations bloomed into a non-playlist, freewheeling, and outspoken voice for the hippie generation that would rival even Pacifica Radio. Larry Yurdin actually almost convinced Pacifica FM station WBAI in New York's legendary and unorthodox radio personality Bob Fass to join WPLJ's air staff. Fass, who years earlier had pioneered freeform radio with his nightly program, "Radio Unnameable," thought better of it and remained at WBAI.

Very positive, yet skeptical, reviews poured in from the underground press in all markets. It was hard for most people, including myself at times, to reconcile the clear incongruity of an establishment network like ABC broadcasting such programming. This contrast was dramatized by Larry Yurdin's office at ABC Headquarters at 1330 Avenue of the Americas. All offices in the forty-story building were painted white. The ABC art department had prescribed and provided thousands of glass framed prints of innocuous subject matter for the walls of each office. Larry Yurdin had hung East Indian blankets with colorful psychedelic patterns from his ceiling and on the walls of his office. When you entered this sanctum, the effect was that of a tent. Yurdin's office raised more than one eyebrow among the corporate types at the network, but nobody ever asked us to take the blankets down.

NOTES

1. *Life*, December 26, 1969, p. 72.

2. Charles R. Morris, *A Time of Passion* (New York: Penguin Books, 1986), p. 81.

3. Terry H. Anderson, *The Movement and the Sixties* (New York: Oxford University Press, 1995), p. 241.

4. Theodore Roszak, *The Making of the Counter Culture* (New York: Doubleday, 1969), p. 16.

5. Ibid., pp. 23, 26.

6. Ibid., p. 155.

7. David Caute, *The Year of the Barricades: A Journey Through 1968* (New York: Harper and Row, 1988), p. 36.

8. Ibid., p. xiii.

9. Jim Ladd, *Radio Waves: Life and Revolution on the FM Dial* (New York: St. Martin's Press), p. 5.

10. *Wall Street Journal*, April 1991, 18.

11. Bruce Morrow, *Cousin Brucie: My Life in Rock and Roll Radio* (New York: Beech Tree Books, 1987), p. 175.

12. Allan Parachini, "The Aging Legacy of Woodstock," *Los Angeles Times*, June 18, 1989, p. 4.

13. Annie Gottlieb, *Do You Believe in Magic?* (New York: Times Books, 1987), p. 39.

14. Eric Rhoads, interview with the author, June 1995.

15. Lynda Crawford, *East Village Other*, March 11, 1971, p. 9.

16. Steve Post, "Son of Play List: The Decline and Fall of Commercial Free Form Radio," *Village Voice*, October 14, 1971, p. 49.

17. Peter B. Orlik, *The Electronic Media* (Boston: Allyn and Bacon, 1992), p. 193.

18. Peter Fornatale and Joshua Mills, *Radio in the Television Age* (New York: Overlook Press, 1980), p. 131.

19. Mike Harrison, ed., *The AOR Story* (Los Angeles: Radio and Records Publishing, 1978), p. 38.

20. Anderson, *The Movement*, p. 246.

21. Susan Krieger, *Hip Capitalism* (Hollywood: Sage Publications, 1979), p. 100.

22. Anderson, *The Movement*, p. 256.

23. Morrow, *Cousin Brucie*, p. 176.

24. Caute, *Year of the Barricades*, p. 37.

25. Suzanne Labin, *Hippies, Drugs and Promiscuity* (New Rochelle, NY: Arlington House, 1972), p. 160.

Chapter Three

The Sound that Rebounds, Resounds, and Rebounds

The radio was screaming "Power to the People—Right On!"
—Hunter S. Thompson

By describing the underground format as the antidote to Top 40, Tom Donahue wanted to make it amply clear to everyone that things were being done quite differently at his station. In fact, not only did he reject the notion of labeling things (such as underground, freeform, progressive), he felt the term "format" itself had little to do with his new brand of radio. Calling it the "anti-format" format, however, would not have offended him quite as much. Nonetheless, there was a plan, a design, behind his seemingly pell-mell approach to station programming.

> *Raechel Donahue:* There was a strategy and purpose, of course. There always is behind something successful. What would happen is he would think it up, and I would lay it down. I was Archie to his Nero Wolfe. He was a triple Gemini. I'm a triple Virgo, and we complemented each other nicely. As his partner in crime, he knew I would implement his ideas in the way he wanted. "Do it the way I would do it, not the way you would do it if you were me," he'd say. It's a subtle difference, but therein lies the secret to why it worked.

> *John Gehron:* They had almost no structure and bragged about it to their listeners. The underground stations threw out all of the Top 40 format rules and on-air sounds because they were against the establishment in all forms.

In a *Rolling Stone* article written the same year Donahue debuted his programming concept at KMPX, he reluctantly applied the term "format" to explain the essence of his unique approach. "It is a format that embraces the best of today's rock and roll, folk, traditional and city blues, ragae, electronic music, and some jazz and classical selections."[1]

Although Donahue would concede that anything with even an implied structure may be said to possess some kind of form, and therefore a format as applied to radio programming, his central point was that the deejays at his station ultimately shaped what went out over the air. They were the creators and curators of the sound.

Echoing Donahue's position, Julius Lester drew an astute picture of the radio genre. "It's a place where the program producer is free to do whatever he wants—play records, talk, take phone calls on the air, eat his dinner, belch, etc. . . . Freeform radio is an art form. The airwaves are the empty canvas, the producer is the artist, and the sound is the paint."[2]

Decades later, when Donahue alumnus Ben Fong-Torres wrote about his former employer, it could well have served as a description for all undergound radio operations of the time. "Back in the early '70's, KSAN ('Jive 95') was the hippest of all stations and, among young listeners, the only spot on the dial worth tuning in. It was freeform, free-for-all radio; intensely personal and political; outrageous and unpredictable, much like the '60's scene that inspired its birth."[3]

FIRST, THE MELODY

The jukebox with a heart—in FM stereo . . .

It was music, however, that most defined, and at the same time distinguished, underground stations from the rest of the pack on either radio band—AM or FM. Music was the prime element of the genre's esoteric mix—the compound or sacred ingredient that made synthesis possible. It was the axis of the underground sphere.

Ed Shane: There was a mystique that surrounded these stations. As if some private, magic door had been found to a new dimension, members of the audience told each other about it. The word of mouth was amazing. I can't remember anybody who didn't love the music and who didn't want to share it with the audience.

Roland Jacopetti: What I loved most about the programming was its eclecticism—the fact that there were no dos and don'ts. The first time I even heard the music of the Andes was on Bob McClay's show, and I've been a fan of it ever since.

Thom O'Hair: The music would be the first of the program ingredients that would make the underground format distinctive, and that music was from everywhere—folk, jazz, blues, and rock and roll. Keep in mind that this was a time when music was undergoing a hell of a big change. Musicians and song writers were finding their voice to speak about what was happening in the world. Lyrics were addressing more than teen angst, fast cars, and black leather jackets. That's what gave it its edge. The songs spoke about an unjust world, freedom from oppression, and doing your own thing, whatever that might be. It provided a Morse code you could dance to and, most importantly, it scared the shit out of your parents. All that wonderful music, and the old, nearly forgotten folk and blues cats were finding a new audience, with their music being recorded by the stars of the day. There was a fantastic amount of meaningful stuff being pressed and distributed, which was a break from the decade-long flood of pop drool singles.

Larry Miller: The variety was impressive. At KMPX, I'd air artists like Screamin' Jay Hawkins and Louis Jordan, maybe some early Elvis and the Rolling Stones. I'd also intermingle an appropriate Lenny Bruce routine, a classical piece, hard rock, or maybe something from a local band.

Eclectic was the word that best described the presentation of music on underground stations. In his memoir about his days at KSAN, Scoop Nisker writes that the station aired music without regard to category or genre and

in sublime segues and sets of sounds that took listeners on soaring, imaginative musical flights. . . . I remember deejay Edward Bear, one freeform night on KSAN, playing a Buffalo Springfield tune that segued into a Mozart sonata, which he then mixed in and out of a Balinese gamelon piece—the counterpoints cross-culturally counter pointing with each other—and then resolved the whole set with some blues from John Lee Hooker.[4]

This musical ecumenicism was evident at underground stations around the country. For instance, in Detroit, WABX worked diligently to break the standard musical mode found everywhere in radio. Observed underground aficionado Mike Gormley, "The programming at 'ABX is creative and unpredictable. There's a lot of rock but every other kind of music gets played with it. Whatever works for the mood, idea or theme the on-air man is developing."[5]

> *Allen Shaw:* This eclecticism was inspired by Tom Donahue and Tom Gamache. Their novel programming approach influenced the people who implemented commercial underground FM around the country between 1967 and 1970. Music played on these stations was certainly free-form and diverse. It ran the gamut from old blue blues to rhythm and blues, jazz, folk, East Indian, as well as the emerging progressive rockers, like Cream, Hendrix, Jefferson Airplane, and the Grateful Dead.

> *Raechel Donahue:* You know, prior to 1967, there was no rock and roll station on the FM band. That changed with the arrival of KMPX. While the Top 40 stations were playing the ill-conceived "It's a Happening" by the Supremes, we were playing "R-E-S-P-E-C-T" by Aretha Franklin. In the beginning we didn't play Motown, which set us apart from other stations, and we played protest music, which was politically incorrect for mainstream radio.

Were it not for the outcropping of underground stations, many rock artists (some of whom would later became prominent fixtures of the music scene) may have gone unnoticed. "Many groups and artists heard on WPLO-FM are almost never heard on AM stations: The Bob Seeger System, Peter Sarstedt, Procol Harum, Leonard Cohen, Rejoice, The Ultimate Spinach, The Mothers of Invention, Spirit, Country Joe and the Fish, and many others, including Cream and the Doors."[6]

> *Larry Miller:* Plenty of folk rock, filled with cogent messages about the times, got on the air. Later on, these stations played a lot of real soul music, too. Things that weren't heard anywhere got their day on underground. For example, Tony Pigg was the first deejay to play the Dead's "Viola Les Blues." It was one of the no-no long cuts from a group way outside the traditional radio fold, but it got on at KMPX.

I debuted Steve Miller's "Children of the Future." New and ignored music had an outlet finally.

Scott Muni: We all did our own thing, which meant diversity. I did things with British music, for instance, so I got plenty of service from recording companies over there. This music, mostly album stuff, gave my show a real distinctiveness and gave the listening audience something fresh for a change.

The "no-no long cuts" referred to above by Larry Miller were the primary staple of underground radio's music catalog.

Ed Shane: The LP, with its lengthier cuts, was where we went for the sounds that really made us what we were.

A 1969 article in Atlanta's *Metro Beat Magazine* commended Shane for taking this step at WPLO-FM:

Ed's formula for success is to program long play albums much more than other Atlanta stations. He plays the best songs from the albums most of which are not put out as singles nor heard on other stations. Success formula number 2 of Ed and WPLO-FM is their primary concern in entertaining and not selling records. Sales don't matter to Ed. "If it's a good record, it should be played," he told us. Too many "good" records are stuffed on a shelf somewhere because they are never heard . . . because they are not selling . . . because they are not heard. This is a cycle upon which Ed has declared war.[7]

Dan Carlisle: This huge amount of album music by bands like the Stones, Beatles, et cetera, had no outlet. The fan was buying albums, but the radio station was playing singles. Then there was the long song—the Doors and their seven-minute "Light My Fire," the Beatles and their concept albums and tracks that ran together for a seamless twenty-minute music experience, and other bands like the Dead and Hendrix, who just confused the gatekeepers.

SCHEMADDICTS

Groovin' with the people on revolution radio . . .

The way in which music was presented by undergrounders was unlike that by any other contemporary radio station. Interestingly, if not ironically, these new outlets did reflect an older adult format, which was responsible for bringing the FM band to a larger audience in the 1960s. Its name was Beautiful Music or, as many called it, "elevator music." It was the Muzak format of the radio world. The common ground between the two seemingly disparate forms of radio programming was the manner in which they structured music into sweeps—that is, uninterrupted segments or blocks, typically of a quarter hour in length. Evolving from the sweep approach was the idea of music sets, wherein a series of songs would establish a particular theme or motif.

> *Roland Jacopetti:* Integration was always important, putting together uninterrupted blocks of music in sets that connected and made a musical statement. The ideal being that at the end of fourteen minutes of music thousands of listeners would collectively say "Wow!"

> *Larry Miller:* The precedent of programming music in sets was already established, for example in jazz radio formats. We just adapted it to playing rock. Sweeping did help separate us from the other commercial outlets. That is, playing music in sets of fifteen, or twenty, or thirty minutes at a time, when almost all other radio stations were doing song/break, song/break. When we finally did get spots, we naturally maintained the music sets and then did spots in clusters or groupings. This hadn't been done before on contemporary music stations. "Double-spotting" was a cardinal sin, and we did up to four spots at a time. We got killer ratings eventually because we were sweeping a lot of people past the quarter hour points, although at the time we didn't even realize that we were doing it.

> *Raechel Donahue:* Again, we played music the way people did in their homes. In the beginning, we played sets of three songs by one artist or three songs that had a theme or some sort of connection. One of our favorite specialties was the "round," in which you might segue Aretha's "Respect," Otis Redding's "Respect," Otis' "Satisfaction," the Stones' "Satisfaction," the Stones' "Red Rooster," and Willie Dixon's "Red Rooster," and so on, until you would work your way back to Aretha. If you were driven, this could take up your whole show. To do something like that took incredible musical knowledge, not to mention a somewhat twisted mind.

> *Dusty Street:* A twisted mind was a definite asset. At the top of the hour, when I came on, I'd have a couple of records

in mind, but my entire set would evolve from those records. That, of course, is very different from today, and it was novel in radio back then, too. Deejays don't put playlists together anymore. We'd pour a lot of energy in devising mixes. In format radio, the air people are provided with lists put together by the program director with the aid of a computer. I think one of the best things about being involved in underground radio at that time was the relationship we had with the music industry. Because we didn't categorize ourselves in any particular format niche, all the recording companies felt we represented an opportunity for them.

Dwight Douglas: PDs actually wanted to hear your sets. The term "set" was taken from live musical performances in clubs. A set was all the songs a band played between each break, and in radio a set might last fifteen to thirty minutes. This demanded long backsells [recaps] of all the songs, artists, and LP titles, much like public radio does in their classical shows today. The backsell traditionally started with the song most recently played backwards to the first song of the set. It was a more music, less talk approach not dissimilar in that respect to what the Beautiful Music stations were doing.

The system of archiving and cataloging such a diverse array of music at underground stations could be complex, to say the least, and assumed many forms—or, in some cases, it was amorphous.

Raechel Donahue: It seemed like everybody had their own idea about how to organize the station's albums and music. We had a system at KMPX and KSAN that was based on Tom's concept of the on-air music mix. It was 60 percent "thread of the familiar," that is to say, mainstream, 20 percent blues and R&B, 10 percent jazz, and 10 percent spoken word and electronic music. When introducing new music, we always encased it in a familiar setting—putting it in the middle of the set—so that listeners wouldn't balk. We had a big discussion with one woman who was helping us organize the library because she wanted to file the black artists separately. Tom solved the whole thing by asking her, "Then where would you put Mose Allison?" Moreover, we decided that Pink Floyd should be under "P," since it wasn't anyone's name, but we decided that T-Bone

Walker should be under "W." After big stations picked up on our format in the seventies, they had fits trying to file Lynyrd Skynyrd.

Ed Shane: To say the music libraries at these stations were all over the place would be an understatement. One thing you can say is that they were usually huge, due mostly to the fact that the air staff had such a considerable knowledge and interest in music. The people on the air knew what was new and who was playing it. We had to, because the audience either knew already or wanted to learn from us. And people in the audience would contribute, bring[ing] records they had picked up in other cities or telling us about artists they had heard elsewhere. We made sure we could get our hands on not only the Beatles' version of "Roll Over Beethoven," but Chuck Berry's original as well. Not just the Rolling Stones' "Not Fade Away," but Buddy Holly's too. Then there was the derivative stuff. What had Steve Winwood done before he formed Traffic? We played the Spencer Davis Group as the answer. Where did the Allman Brothers Band come from? We played Hour Glass as the answer, and so on. And the writers—not just Joe Cocker's "Bird on the Wire," but Leonard Cohen's recording also. If we could find no theme apparent in the lyric, we looked for one in the presentation of the music. For example, flute to flute or mandolin to mandolin. Did song number one end in a key compatible with the first few notes of song number two? If so, we used it to create a seamless listening experience. Of course, all of this required vast resources of music. The air staff had to establish a strong relationship with the station's music library. A visceral and intellectual correspondence had to be there. The air talent could use the library to their advantage, sharing information about the artists and the music. When hiring for the air, we looked for people who had a real affinity for the music. In a way they were musicologists, whose schooling was the concert venues and record stores, augmented by *Rolling Stone* and other music magazines.

Roland Jacopetti: You'd hear about all sorts of methods for managing the music inventory at freeform stations. We had a red dot file of frequently played classics just outside the control room door, and the entire record library was a few feet down the hall. That seemed to make sense to me, a way of exerting a certain order and influence, while still respecting the ability of each jock to be a skillful music programmer.

Kate Ingram: We kept it simple enough, using index cards. They'd be categorized and color-coded. It wasn't brain surgery.

UNDERGROUND PLAYLIST SAMPLERS AND STATEMENT

Wrap your legs around the radio . . .

KSAN-FM (San Francisco)

Sample cuts from Tom Donahue's playlist between 1968 and 1972:

"Darkness, Darkness," The Youngbloods

"I'd Love to Change the World," Ten Years After

"On the Road Again," Canned Heat

"What About Me?" Quicksilver Messenger Service

"Scottish Tea," The Amboy Dukes

"Fresh Garbage," Spirit

"Time Has Come Today," The Chambers Brothers

"So You Want to Be a Rock 'n' Roll Star," The Byrds

"Shoot Out on the Plantation," Leon Russell

"Delta Lady," Joe Cocker

"Hurdy Gurdy Man," Donovan

KSHE-FM (St. Louis)

Most frequently played artists (late 1960s and early 1970s): Cream, Moody Blues, Leon Russell, Neil Young, Santana, Lou Reed, Rolling Stones, Spirit, Traffic, Steppenwolf, Pink Floyd, Lynyrd Skynyrd, Iron Butterfly, Humble Pie, Led Zeppelin, Jefferson Airplane, Emerson, Lake, and Palmer, The Doors, Buffalo Springfield, Deep Purple, Janis Joplin, Spencer Davis, Allman Brothers, Uriah Heep, Ten Years After.

WPLJ-FM (New York)

The following memo, sent by the station's program director to the on-air staff in 1971, outlines his playlist approach. By this time, the mechanics of program formatics were becoming evident at many album rock stations, especially those owned by large corporations such as ABC. The days of the freeform, "do your own thing" approach to music selection were quickly fading.

TO: Talent
FROM: Mitchell Weiss
SUBJECT: Program Aids

We currently have three record lists. There is an A list of hit singles. There is a B list of currently popular albums. Both the A and the B lists appear on the first page of the copy book for your show and will be changed every Wednesday. There is a C list of standard progressive rock oldies also. This list at this time is in your heads and includes familiar tracks of Dylan, Beatles, Stones, etc. In the next few days, we should have a C list available to you.

Basically we are asking you to use these program aids in the following way. Our revised Daily Music Playlist should be used for planning out each hour of your show. The key time zones—:00, :15, and :45 (indicated by the dot) should be filled with A, B, C track. All the selections you play either in or not in the key zones should be marked in the box at the far right by an A, B, C or an N for recommended tracks from new records. If the track is not in any of these categories, only then should the box be left empty. In the daytime there should be a minimum total of four B tracks. In our discussions I mentioned how these numbers vary at other times. In a four day period, you should have played every item on the A list at least once.

We will be having weekly music meetings on Tuesday to discuss new records, recommended tracks, and the A, B, and C lists.

As the use of these aids develops, you should expect some refinements and alterations from time to time. For instance, we are seriously contemplating narrowing down the B list as well as designing some kind of master chart for the B list to allow you to see at a glance the distribution of B record play prior to your show. We are also thinking how best to show you the exposure of recommended tracks from new records prior to your show. We are also setting up a research system to insure that our B list is based on a variety of inputs, not just a trade paper chart number, or one record store's sales figures, or five phone calls to the studio; but as many objective inputs as possible, including our own judgement. If you are still unclear about any of the details in the use of our program aids, or the reason behind them, please feel free to ask me about them.

Thanks for your cooperation.

TALKING HEADS

Grooving with the Air Aces . . .

Just as the approach to music programming in underground was antithetical to conventional AM radio, particularly Top 40, announcing styles were no less contrary to the long-standing norm. Since the medium's inception in the early 1920s, announcing techniques have undergone relatively subtle changes, never wandering too far from the affected "radioese" presentation style (in recent years parodied by Phil Hartman, Gary Owens, and Don Pardo) typified by the likes of Harold Arlin, H. V. Kaltenborn, Lowell Thomas, Gabriel Heatter, Boake Carter, Edward R. Murrow, and so on. The old-line announcer style, characterized by its formality and self-consciousness, remained prevalent well into the second coming of the radio medium, which followed the arrival of television.

The "stilts," as they have been called, found their way into the FM band as well, migrating to the Beautiful Music format and others. In fact, they had been there all along, performing the various announcing chores required of the "fine arts" alternative medium—"And now we take you back to symphony hall for the second act of Verdi's magnificent opera, Aïda." However, in fairness to early FM announcers, there was an attempt to shed a modicum of AM's microphone histrionics and to attenuate the hyperbolic enunciation and projection so rampant at the pop music and top-of-the-chart outlets.

The underground radio voice would bring this early effort to militate against the disingenuous affectations and mannerisms—the hype—on the airwaves to a fuller realization.

> *Charles Laquidara:* For one thing, and this is kinda key, we didn't think of ourselves as radio announcers or deejays. We were ourselves, guys who communicated as individuals, not radio personas. Deejays were those fucking hype-heads on AM Top 40.

Wrote underground broadcaster Scoop Nisker, "Everybody was playing with their identities, dressing up, and trying to trip one another out. We wanted to become new people, born again in the Age of Aquarius."[8]

> *Dave Dixon:* Perhaps, but above all we were out to be who we were on the air. We talked normal, not like the CKLW stilts. We were never asked to be hyped or affected. Being conversational and real was our goal.
>
> *Mike Harrison:* We were laid-back, but in a hippie flavor. That's where we were. It was our milieu.
>
> *Ed Shane:* There was an implictly prescribed way of presenting yourself. Announcing styles were to be subdued and super-intimate. Very conversational. The announcer could be straight as hell as long as he sounded like he knew what he was talking about.
>
> *Lee Abrams:* I think the goal was to sound as mellow and different from the other radio voices on the dial as possible. The idea was to be kind of an anti-announcer announcer.

In her reflection on the underground sound in the *New York Times*, Karen Schoemer cites Tom Donahue as the ultimate model or exemplar of the programming genre's announcing style.

> He is remembered for his bass voice, big and rumbling, yet soothing, floating on a foundation of absolute authority. While FM jocks of the late '60's sounded like what they often were, that is, stoned, Donahue (whatever state he might have been in) had his act together. He was hip without trying.[9]

On the latter point, industry publisher Eric Rhoads acknowledges that the "stoned" radio announcer persona projected by underground stations was often an integral part of the radio genre's presentation. "The personalities were soft-spoken, low key and sounded stoned (most probably were). . . . [It] was loose."[10]

> *Russ Gibb:* Part of this whole thing was to sound "with it." I think the very fact that our emphasis was on doing things slowly set us apart from the rest of the radio market. We coughed a lot, which was an attempt to convey the sense that we were all doing marijuana. Lotsa hip, inside jokes

that our listeners were in on added to this. We wanted to sound real cool, so we used plenty of hip jargon, too.

Top 40 maven Bruce Morrow offered his unique, if not cynical, perspective on the subject in his autobiography:

The best FM announcers sounded like they'd been awakened from a deep sleep, as if they could hardly concentrate long enough to read a spot before they nodded off. . . . Where AM radio screamed about drag strips and twist lounges, FM told you in confidence that they knew where the party was. . . . Where the most successful jocks on AM sounded like they'd love a piece of your bubble gum, the rising stars of FM sounded like they knew where you kept your stash of pot. . . . Better to let the long-hair jocks, who talked as if they were walking through pudding, play what the hippies and yippies wanted to hear.[11]

Dan Carlisle: Sure, the guys on underground were into themselves and into their own world. Admittedly, they were a totally self-indulgent lot, and sounded like it to many outsiders, but could it have been any other way? When you point someone toward a studio and tell him to fill four hours of radio time the way he sees fit, what do you expect?

Raechel Donahue: Yeah, the jocks were among the most self-absorbed and indulgent out there. Certainly, at least in the beginning that was true. But they knew what their audience wanted. That shouldn't be overlooked. We used to have weekly meetings and we would go over everyone's shows to see if any of us were banging on one particular drum too long. Ultimately, I think the sound everyone was after had to do with sincerity. Not faking it, that is.

John Gorman: That was true, at least, in the beginning, but as the format matured, talent became overly self-impressed, and that behavior is insidious. A lot of the on-air people got the fame buzz, and when that happens . . . well, you know the rest.

THE ELEMENTS

All the news that's fit to rip . . .

As with all radio stations, there are other ingredients besides the music and announcing that contribute to their general appeal, identity, and overall listenability. News and information broadcasts represent one of those elements. Despite the underground programming genre's dominant emphasis on album music designed for an under-thirty crowd, it differed from other youth-oriented music outlets in that news was frequently regarded as an integral part of what many of these stations sought to convey to their public. That is, they wished to be construed as members of the socially conscious media community and not simply record machine operators.

The prevailing form that radio news assumed after the introduction of programming specialization in the 1950s and 1960s was the five-minute update, usually at the top of the hour. Because the FCC required that broadcasters dedicate a percentage of their schedules to news and public affairs, even stations targeting the youth demographic were obliged to stop the music and air the news. The idea at these stations was to deal with the perceived "tune-out factor" as quickly and as innocuously as possible. "Kids want to hear the hot hits, not what's happening in the world," was the familiar refrain at pop chart stations. Meanwhile, at those outlets promoting "more music and less talk"—like Beautiful Music, the disdain for news obligations was no less in evidence.

> *Ed Shane:* Despite the fact that we were targeting an eighteen- to twenty-seven-year-old audience, news was a central element of our mix. Our listeners were typically in college, and they were fed up with the robot-sounding stations they'd lived with for so long. These people grew up with rock and roll but found that rock radio did not grow up with them, and it was not just the music that frustrated them.

> *Mike Harrison:* This age group in the 1960s was very politically engaged. They were also overtly anti-Vietnam, and they wanted to know what was happening, because it affected their lives.

> *Dusty Street:* We knew this, and we completely directed our news broadcasts toward these concerns. It made us all the more relevant. Our news guys were long-haired, pot-smoking, politically conscious, ultra-liberal, left-wing folk, which pretty much mirrored our audience. Rush Limbaugh would have dropped dead in waltz time if he had heard any of our newscasts.

> *Thom O'Hair:* KSAN had what was called the "Gnus" department. At first the schedule of newscasts was pretty thin and arbitrary. As PD I had concluded that our morning

A box of LOVE . . . tapes.

audience was as interested in news and information as that tuning AM, so I proposed that a member of the Gnus department begin airing newscasts at 7 A.M. Fat chance, was the reaction. When I first brought it up to McQueen and the Gnus crew, I was told that they started their day with the noon news. That's the way Donahue had done it, and no asshole from Oregon was going to tell them different. That kind of reaction was in the main. Since I was PDing the place, I could have ordered them to do it, but that was not the way I worked, nor was it consistent with the spirit around KSAN. So we talked and talked, and time went by. I recall walking along Montgomery Street, the "Wall Street" of San Francisco, one sunny day. The radio studios were nearby, and I needed some fresh air. I had not banked on a revelation, but one did occur. Groups of people were sitting about eating their lunches, and they were tuned to the noon Gnus on KSAN, which was a curiosity in itself, since so few people owned portable FM radios back then. Anyway, I observed this over the course of several days. There they were tuned to the Gnus, which often ran fifteen or twenty minutes. When it was over, to my surprise, I noticed some people changing stations. I couldn't resist asking them why, and they told me they tuned the station primarily for the Gnus, and then expressed the wish that the station aired Gnus in the morning when they were getting ready for the work day—bingo!! The next move was to get McQueen to let somebody else to do the 'cast and come out to lunch with me. This accomplished, we went walking. What he witnessed knocked him out. The same scenario. People tuned to the Gnus who wanted morning coverage too. That did it. We worked it out, did some money shifting, and I had a Gnuscast twice an hour in the mornings. It was a KSAN first, one of many. The ratings and time spent listening went into the double digits with Gnus coverage on Jive 95. In fact, it became the crowning feature of KSAN, one of the main reasons listeners took the station seriously. The news was from the left side of the street and championed the "Everyman" in all of our listeners—no matter the gender. It was the People's Gnus to the little guy getting screwed by the system. During this period there were many big stories unfolding. The war in Vietnam was the biggest, and as history has shown, the bottom-line story was not being told to Mr. and Mrs. America. To stop this unjust war, to bring home the troops, was the goal and motivation behind our newscast. Thursday was body-count day. It was when the government released its casualty figures for the prior week, and it was so much bullshit. Copy like "12,765 dirty, godless commies dead and 10 allies and 4 American troops." During those dark days for truth, there were few voices not singing the government's propaganda song, and much to its lasting credit, the KSAN Gnus department was one of them. KPFA was the other beacon of truth and the other main voice in the Bay Area telling the untold story of 'Nam on the air. There is one thing that I want to put on the record here. It's about the way the news was slanted, and all reporting is slanted, but we never—despite all accusations to the contrary—put the responsibility for the war on the shoulders of the servicemen. They were never referred to as baby killers or any other nasty epithet, and nobody called for people to spit on returning soldiers. The fault was laid at the feet of the political system, right where history has placed it.

The most common form of radio news at the time (as today) consisted of a couple of minutes of world and national stories and a minute or so of local and regional stories. This was typically followed by a commercial break, a sports recap, and a brief weather forecast. Immediately after that, the records spun until the top of the next hour. Underground stations broke this ancient mold and dared to try something new.

Scoop Nisker: I'd do interpretive collages of news, replete with opinions.

Dan Carlisle: At KSAN, Scoop took a very alternative approach to news broadcasts. From my perspective, he did the best and most original radio news around. His was not a rip 'n read presentation.

Tim Powell: We rewrote the news copy at WABX, editorializing as we saw fit. For example, instead of using the slanted and politically charged term "Viet Cong," we would change the word to "revolutionaries" or "North Vietnamese." We used neutral words instead of ones used to inflame listeners. Not exactly what I'd call a call to action, but a form of action nonetheless. We did an editorial asking that the marijuana prohibition be rethought. In retrospect, that was like playing a favorite record to our audience. News was designed to push the right buttons, too.

In *Hip Capitalism*, Susan Krieger observed that a news or public service item sometimes amounted to little more than an announcer indicating that an incoming plane carrying drugs had been cancelled that night. Other critics of underground news often found it equally frivolous, self-serving, and wanting.

> *Robert Hilliard:* I was at the FCC when Commissioners Nick Johnson and Ken Cox pushed for a public service (news) percentage requirement for stations. I felt that those PDs and DJs who said their young rock music listeners didn't want to hear news were hypocrites. Especially during this period pop music listeners not only wanted to hear news, and made life decisions, such as enlisting to fight in Nam, reporting for the draft, or going to Canada, based on the news. These PDs and DJs underestimated and denigrated the intelligences and interests of American youth.

> *Thom O'Hair:* I don't know. It seems to me that we took nonmusical elements very seriously. We had public affairs programming unlike anyone had ever heard before—the Gay Show, the Gay News, with the Most Reverend Ray Brouhers (not sure of the exact spelling), the first Drug Report. That show allowed listeners to send a sample of their drugs to Pharm-Chem, using a four-digit code. They would then call the lab and find out just what the drug was. We'd carry the results on the air. Believe it or not, this was a real public service.

> *John Gorman:* Our public service announcements were not your ordinary run-of-the-mill stuff either. They were centered and meaningful to where we were coming from. For example, it was not unusual to run SDS [Students for a Democratic Society] psa's on WNTN.

When it came to promoting underground stations, every effort was made to create an image that conveyed hipness. This strategy was amply apparent at KSAN, where the morning deejay, Bob Prescott, read from the I Ching and aired offbeat features—thick with sound effects—highly editorialized newscasts, and bizarre contests, all especially geared to advance the underground radio image and cause.

Cleveland's premier rocker.

Al Wilson: Promotions and contests were designed to reflect the message of the music, so they usually were music-based. We'd have festivals and concerts. We were doing what became known as lifestyle marketing, and we didn't know it, because we were out to establish continuity in everything we did. Our bumper stickers and t-shirts echoed our programming gestalt. G.I. dog tags with our logo on them said something about our attitude concerning the Vietnam War, and so on.

Mike Harrison: These stations really worked at being hip. It was their raison d'être. A cool image was the programming goal.

Larry Miller: Hip, as pertains to these stations, was a relative term, though. From where I was at back then, hip was defined as "enlightened awareness," and I think that's what was sought and often existed. During the early 1960s, there was a hip underground movement in the country. People who listened to folk, jazz, blues, classical, and foreign music and people who read Kerouac, Pynchon, Ginsberg, and others, were in search of hip. I've always thought of this as a search for authenticity, which would explain why folk and jazz would wind up on the same record shelf. We also dug Ken Nordine, Lord Buckley, and Lenny Bruce—poets and comedians. A lot of it had its roots in eastern religion and philosophy. Kerouac's fusion of East and West in novels like *On the Road*, *The Dharma Bums*, and *The Subterraneans* pointed the way and permeated the ambience at underground stations.

Dave Pierce: Undergrounders dripped with hip. It was everywhere in evidence. That was the idea. Things like satiric and humorous bits were produced to enhance this image. We'd use sound effects, homemade jingles, sound bites from TV news, bootleg tapes to get this idea across.

Dan Carlisle: Production values were carefully considered for their contribution to the overall flow and feel. For instance, station breakers basically followed the same philosophy applied to music and commercials. To get the station calls between cuts of a sweep we might fade up slowly on the sound of an advancing marching band and then at the point when the band is foreground, a voice would chime in with "A-B-X." We'd then gradually fade the band and segue to the next song. All of this was in keeping with our programming objective.

Allen Shaw: A huge amount of effort was invested in production that related the way these stations wished to be identified to the listening public. There was an attitude that these stations worked hard at getting across.

UNCHAINED MELODIES

People's Liberation Radio . . .

There never had been a commercial radio format that gave its practitioners the opportunity to plumb their creative depths as did underground. At the time (and even more so today), radio was programmed very pragmatically and scientifically to ensure its reaching the objective most desired by its owners and entrepreneurs. To double paraphrase the great Bard, revenue was the thing—the quintessence of everything—to commercial station operators, but more on this theme later.

As the television era progressed, on-air people found that their duties were increasingly becoming robotic in nature—button pressing and liner-card announcing. Top 40 had been "Draked" (programmer Bill Drake had tightened the format to deemphasize deejay presence), and adult music stations were being automated to the wall. At other stations, networks and syndicators filled schedules with the Arthur Godfreys and Don McNeills of the day. The local radio personality was being squeezed out of the picture, or so it seemed, when underground radio came along.

Dave Pierce: We were free to talk politics, ecology, drugs, whatever, and program our own music, too, when the transition kicked in at KPPC in 1968. This was truly liberated and liberating radio. I was program director, and I let my air staff alone. The further out and freakier they got, the better. Nobody was really in control in the traditional sense. It was like an extended family at times. Kids of jocks running around, long-haired people hanging out, your old lady (wife or girlfriend) pulling your music.

Russ Gibb: Compared to other radio, it was a pretty wild scene, I suppose. We looked pretty shaggy with our long hair and bell bottoms. We would stand out, and we were often ridiculed by the public. It wasn't uncommon for bands to hang out at the station or with jocks. Artists like

Eric Clapton and Janis Joplin would linger around. It was real open space. The AM guys were on another planet, one with lots of fences.

Ed Shane: This freedom inspired spontaneity. We'd do live interviews with artists as they dropped by. Our tiny studio in Atlanta had no room for musical performances, so we had artists play "guest deejay," choosing their favorite cuts from our library. Duane Allman chose John Coltrane, Joe Cocker played Beatles cuts to try and disprove the "Paul is dead" rumors, Mick Fleetwood spun Elmore James to demonstrate the bluesman's influence on Fleetwood Mac. Studio space was larger at WGLD in Chicago, so we often had acoustic performances with musicians gathered around one microphone. I taped John Hartford, Steve Goodman, John Prine, and others. I had Jane Fonda and Holly Near sing live on our air on behalf of the McGovern presidential campaign. Anytime I could get a live performance on the air, I did. I felt that was a real unique aspect of the format that no Top 40 station would ever try to copy. In Chicago, we presented a Carly Simon acoustic set from a downtown club, only to be accused by her manager of tainting the performance by broadcasting it on a non-union station.

Thom O'Hair: Thinking back on the drug test controversy at KSAN, the corporation that owned the station [Metromedia] and WNEW, KMET, WMMR, and others, stood behind us in this and other matters. It stood up for the right of free speech. I would like to see the cowards at the helm of NPR and CPB do that today. Sure MM probably did it because we were making money for them, but so what? They were behind us. I can't sufficiently express my respect for the people who ran Metromedia. Men like George Duncan, Jack Thayer, Willis Duff, and John Kluge were real stand-up guys. The fact of the matter is that the "front office" of MM was as important to the success of this form of radio as anybody. At the time I didn't feel that way. Like others, I thought they were just a bunch of old men interfering with us Young Turks down in the radio trenches, but I learned after working for scared little assbites over the years that followed that the upper management team at MM was really strong and unique. It gave us the sacred space necessary for flight.

GOOD CITIZENS AND THOSE BAD BUREAUCRATS

You're on the Big Mattress . . .

What added to the contradictory nature of the term "underground" radio, at least from the perspective of critics like Black Panther leader Eldridge Cleaver, was the fact that these stations usually prided themselves on being conscientious citizens—members of good standing in the community served by their signals. A principle closely adhered to at undergrounds, according to columnist Rex Weiner, was always to "relate to the community" and "make lots of public service announcements."[12]

> *Dusty Street:* We were ultra community-oriented and very proactive. The entire radio station, all of its programming elements, reflected the community we were after. We weren't *targeting* listeners like all the other stations. We were the legitimate voice of the community. What we were doing was reflecting a time and a culture that had no voice until we came along.

In her detailed organizational evaluation of KSAN, Susan Krieger found this to be true, noting that the prime topics of deejays had to do with politics, drugs, and ecology.[13] A survey of other underground station program schedules reveals a strong emphasis on community issues.

> *Ed Shane:* This is one of the things I think that favorably characterized this type of station—a desire to be a real part of the community, to assume some responsibility. In our own unique way we would try to do this whenever possible. We'd be on the air with things that mattered to our listeners. I recall a WPLO press release about our planned election coverage in September 1970. The text is as follows:
>
>> (Atlanta)—WPLO-FM, Progressive Rock outlet here, has announced what the station is calling "non-coverage" of the September 9th election returns.
>>
>> Station operations manager Ed Shane explained that WPLO-FM had pressed into service a team of comedy writers to report on the happenings of "secondary election day" in Georgia.
>>
>> "We plan to give factual coverage of the news events," Shane said. "The WPLO-FM audience will definitely know who's winning and who's losing. We're just adding some-

thing more. We've padded a studio for a makeshift team of itinerant brain pickers to use in order to spoof the cliched Action-Central-Election-Headquarters reporting that radio and TV stations fall into every two years.

"Our writers, including an unemployed door-to-door fired chicken salesman (the voice of 'Captain Wishbone') and Officer Red Baron of the Unidentified Flying Police, have been given strict orders that no fact should be on the air while they are. Otherwise, they have a fairly free hand."

WPLO-FM person Steve Hosford and his steam-operated sound effects machine will act as co-producers of the madness, which is anticipated to strike the air in a thrashing motion twice an hour during the evening.

Dave Pierce: There was a passion for what was going on out there in the community, and it manifested itself in a lot of interesting forms. In the final analysis, however, a significant link existed between the station and its listening constituents.

Flying in the face of this seemingly benevolent behavior was the general view that underground stations were the bad boys—the rogues, if not degenerates—of the radio industry. Admittedly, there were occasions when the FCC and other government agencies raised their eyebrows over some of the events taking place at these nontraditional outlets, but on the whole few enforcement actions were actually initiated.

Thom O'Hair: Things got stirred up occasionally. For instance, the FCC freaked out over our Pharm Chem feature, and they did come down hard across the country on songs with drug references. That created a chill of sorts. It was a bullshit law, so when it was passed we had an all-drug weekend and played everything that was on the taboo list. We read the Bill of Rights between records to make our point. Sure, the FCC made a station live up to its license commitments, and that's what we felt we were doing with our drug report, but it got us into some hot water. In our minds, we were serving the needs of our diverse audience and living up to our community obligations.

KSAN found itself in hot water on more than one occasion. One of the most provocative clashes with the feds had to do with an alleged death threat against Richard Nixon by one of its announcers. On December 3, 1969,

Roland Young repeated over the air a statement made earlier in the day by a Black Panther which advocated the assassination of the president. Within hours special agents were at the station's door, and soon after, Young was fired by Metromedia executives.

Less dramatic confrontations were far more common and mostly centered around reported drug use. On a few occasions, station staff members were arrested for smoking marijuana, which underground air personalities like Ed Bear and Tony Pigg felt was quite unjust, since from their perspective pot enhanced their performances and therefore benefitted their listening audiences.

Stefan Ponek: This would rattle the MM executives. Whenever there was a drug-related incident, such as a deejay being busted for smoking pot, there'd be a series of conferences among the higher-ups about how this would impact profit potential. Most of this drug stuff occurred on the West Coast. The New York guys were very well behaved by comparison.

Krieger notes that KSAN was in trouble with the FCC for allegedly promoting subversive activities by announcing the times and locations of protest meetings centering around the trial of the Chicago Seven. She also cites a clash with the commission over KSAN's airing of a show that graphically focused on oral sex.[14]

The broadcast of obscenity and profanity inspired the ire of the FCC, and when it occurred the station almost always handled the incident with speed and severity as a measure to keep federal officials from initiating retaliatory punitive actions. In 1969 a group of Bard College graduates, calling themselves Spiritus Cheese, put WHFS-FM on the books by featuring "the music and politics of the emerging counterculture; [but] like a number of deejays over the years, they were eventually fired, ostensibly for airing an obscene Firesign Theatre tape."[15]

On the whole, however, the reputation that these stations got for being hotbeds of illegal activity was undeserved.

Allen Myers: Despite the incendiary statements often made by underground personalities, few enforcement actions were ever initiated by the commission, because it was disinclined to become involved or, if you will, enmeshed, in matters of content.

WOR-FM's 1967 POSITIONING STATEMENT

A radio station's positioning statement presents its self-depiction (pro-file). It reveals how the station chooses to be perceived by its targeted audience and advertising clientele. In 1967, when the following statement was prepared, WOR-FM was about to undergo programming changes which would move it closer to a commercial mainstream presentation.

Radio station WOR-FM was born a year ago and within a very short period of time became a big factor in New York metropolitan radio. Its acceptance was almost immediate and from the onset, WOR-FM became highly competitive with AM (not FM) radio.

WOR-FM provided RKO General with:

1. Leadership in the industry
2. A new service to listeners
3. Revenue to absorb operating costs imposed on the company as a result of the divorce from AM radio per the FCC
4. Listenership, and
5. Filling a void in New York which has existed since the emergence of contempory radio.

WOR-FM is . . .

1. Unique
2. Different
3. Accepted
4. Merchandisable
5. Exciting
6. *Needed*

The major appeal of WOR-FM includes the following:

1. It is contemporary music.
2. It is the most accepted music in the country and world today.

and WOR-FM

3. Plays twice as much contemporary music as its competitors.
4. Has greater flexibility in its music than any other station.
5. Exposes material which requires and merits exposure.
6. Has forced competition to be aware of WOR-FM as a major com-petitor through selections of music.
7. Has gained the respect of the industry and allied industries for its awareness of the music scene as it is today and also for its courage to play music which should be played.

ANYTHING WHICH HAS MERIT BASED ON GOOD TASTE

There is no secret formula for WOR-FM music, save for the great amount played, the flexibility in the selection, and the balance achieved through variety.

THE WOR-FM AUDIENCE

WOR-FM strives to reach an audience . . .

1. Which is 18–34 years of age.
2. Which has tired of the screaming, yelling, over-jingled robot radio that has commanded audiences through the years.
3. Which is responsive.
4. Which appreciates quality of presentation.
5. Which does criticize but solely because that audience "feels" the station.
6. Which participates in the station.
7. Which is grateful for WOR-FM.

WOR-FM has succeeded in reaching that audience. The latest figures indicate that overall, in the important seven to midnight audience, WOR-FM is number one in New York for men 18–24.

WOR-FM's audience receives . . .

1. More music than any other station plays in the contemporary field.
2. Music played in stereo with a concentration on quality.
3. Personalities who speak with the audience, not down to it.
4. An intelligent approach to every happening on the station.
5. A limited commercial commitment in order that the programming is not sacrificed.

The WOR-FM personality is . . .

1. Knowledgeable in the music he plays.
2. Different from the personality before him or after him, each one unique in style and delivery.
3. Subdued in his delivery (intelligent approach).
4. Relating to the music he plays.

RATINGS

By and large, radio is a game of ratings, and WOR-FM . . .

1. Has consistently increased its audience from one rating period to the next.

2. Reaches the important audience, the buying audience, the 18–34 year old audience.
3. Has an audience which responds to it and its personalities.
4. Reaches an audience which is extremely loyal to it.

WOR-FM SUMMARY

It would be easy to speak about WOR-FM for hours, but it would take reams of paper.

WOR-FM, through knowledgeable management, looked years ahead to what certainly will represent the contemporary music station. WOR-FM filled a great void which existed in New York. No station in the country would dare present a new concept in contemporary entertainment.

WOR-FM dared and is now reaping the success of its initiative to enter the contemporary field of radio. WOR-FM is distinctive in this field since it is . . .

THE ONLY STATION OF ITS KIND IN AMERICA

WOR-FM strives to reach the 18–34 year old audience. It reaches a teenage audience as well. However, that is not the concentration. Anything below the age of 18 is "gravy" and anything above the age of 34 is "gravy." These are plus-factors.

WOR-FM is reaching the audience it wants . . . the buying audience . . . the spending audience.

For years the theory has been to get the adults you must get the kids . . .

WELL

Those kids are now the adults and they have tired of "Robot Radio," "Hot Rod Radio," "Slam Bang Radio," and "Trite Radio."

The audience has discovered WOR-FM!

For years, contemporary radio has been infected with the malignancy or "Format Radio" . . . time, temp, jingle, record. Tape five minutes of this kind of radio, and you've heard the entire week. It is needed and required in many markets, but this is New York.

If WOR-FM must use the word "formula" or "format," it would be because it insists on:

15 Records per hour

News as scheduled

Public service as scheduled

Commercials as scheduled

From that point on, we desire and concentrate on *Personality.* In this, we find yet another appeal factor. No two people on the staff sound the same on the air. They are different in presentation, in delivery, and are keenly aware of one big factor:

AUDIENCE COMPOSITION

It is a simple "format." Easy to copy by other radio stations, except for one important area, [in] which WOR-FM may claim no competition:

PEOPLE HIGHLY KNOWLEDGEABLE IN MUSIC

Music is, as already stated, the most important ingredient, and every record received at the station is listened to, including both sides.

If a song has merit . . . play it. If a song has controversy but is in good taste . . . play it. The music is handled in an extremely meticulous manner, both in selection and in the way it is aired.

PROJECTION

WOR-FM plans a series of promotional endeavors which will be distinctively different from other contemporary music competitors so that we may again stand apart from them.

The freshening of the air sound will be a constant objective.

There is little doubt that more and more audience will be added to the already over 1 million people tuning in.

There is little doubt that this audience—the buying audience—will reward WOR-FM for its courage and its convictions by responding to advertisers who buy on. This is already happening.

WOR-FM is prepared to submit evidence—published evidence—of America's greatest success story for a new concept in Broadcasting.

WOR-FM . . .

1. Is distinctive

2. Is unique

3. Has over 1 million listeners and growing

4. Is the #1 FM radio station in the country

5. Is in full competition with WMCA and WABC and getting audience from these stations

6. Is commercially active

7. Is accepted

8. Is loved

9. Is appreciated

WOR-FM *IS NEEDED!!*

NOTES FROM THE SOUTHERN UNDERGROUND

The following document was prepared in 1969 by Ed Shane, operations manager of Atlanta underground station WPLO-FM. It served as the station's programming treatise into the early 1970s, when the format was further adjusted to reflect the shifting mood and lifestyles prevalent in the south's largest city.

TO: WPLO-FM Programming Staff:

The announcer should avoid so-called "hip" clichés that come off as only clichés: "dig" . . . "very together" . . . "That's tight" . . . "chick" . . . "gas" . . . and so on.

And above all:

Everything the personality says must, and I emphasize must, relate to the music that's playing. All ad libs, all interviews, all talk not essential to a spot or radio service must be related to the music. The basis for the success of the format is the total involvement with the music. Personalities must, through their attitude and intimacy, achieve with the recorded music what a live band would with instruments and decibels.

Many stations have been confusing the intimate, conversational announcing style with non-professionalism. There is no need to sound lost or to sound so spontaneous that the show sounds thrown together. What you would say in the "attitude" format is so much more important to the overall concept of the show and the music that it should be prepared in advance. In other words, remember your medium—communication. You cannot bumble and effectively communicate.

Commercials should be fewer in number during the attitude format shows. Never double spot! The audience, given this approach, believes you're doing this for its benefit, so that it may hear more music. This should be your intent. You hold your audience while showcasing each spot. That's good for everybody. Spots should be produced separately for the "attitude" format show. They should be toned down and delivered in at a slower pace so as to match the intimacy of surrounding elements. Letting announcers read live copy so that they can be more closely identified with the account supporting the underground sound may be a good idea. Sell, don't pitch copy.

For me it is much more fun to write spots for the attitude format audience than for a general audience. Here you can use every trick in the book. At your disposal [are] humor, satire, poetry, current events, and so forth. Whatever the client will allow, and many will give you free rein. Avoid the notion that some products may be too "establishment" for the audience you're after. Granted, there will be some hardcore listeners who will protest a department store ad or a soft drink spot on the grounds that it is a sell out, but don't worry. You cannot program exclusively for the hardcores out there. If you did, you'd have about three hundred listeners and the weirdest goddamn station in the world.

Regarding public service material, it would be best to avoid the armed services—army, navy, marines, air force. Local psa's are best, but if you use national stuff, go for VISTA or the Peace Corps (both organizations have excellent recorded material that fits well with the attitude format). Money appeals are also bad unless you can tie in with something like the Biafra Relief Fund, or something like that.

Now, about the music!

The music format is simple. There is none, per se! Of course, for reasons of getting the most popular or most requested songs on the air, some sort of record must be kept of what music is being bought at the record stores. Use this as a guide, not the rule as in Top 40. People seem to identify with artists rather than with song, cut, or album title. So if someone wants to hear Al Kooper, many times it will not matter whether you play his new "I Stand Alone" album or some from the "Blues Project." More on this later. Now back to formatics.

Make certain that every second or third selection is something from your controlled list. Something selling, something requested heavily, or a recognizable oldie. This will keep your audience from drifting away from you. Even though you may have to go through a process of educating your listeners about new music and new artists, you must make sure they are given music here and there that they don't have to "work on." Give them a familiar post to lean on, then throw them something fresh. This will acclimatize them.

Balance is very important. Too many underground stations seem to rely on a solid diet of hard rock. A non-stop diet of pounding rock will make a listener a nervous wreck. You are better off using the tried and true "fast/medium/slow" formula that we all learned at our first good music station job. Make it "heavy/medium/light" for our purposes. That is, Iron Butterfly might do a slow song, but they're heavy as hell—an exhausting musical experience! Joplin is the same. These should be balanced with a song that is lighter in texture or arrangement. Two heavies in a row is fine, but make sure you break the sound somewhere. Folk material comes in handy as a breaker. Judy Collins, Buffy Sainte-Marie, Joni Mitchell, Tim Buckley, Tim Hardin, Ritchie Havens, Bob Dylan, Donovan all have their place in this format. Remember, too, that many of the heavies are doing the folk stuff anyway.

When there is no other "attitude" station in a market, you can go after the pop music innovators. The early musicians are as valid today as they were when they broke new ground. I'm talking about 1965–1966 early musicians. This was the period when Stephen Stills and Neil Young were with Buffalo Springfield doing songs like "Rock and Roll Woman," "Go and Say Goodbye," "For What It's Worth," "Clancy Can't Even Sing," "Mr. Soul," "Bluebird," and more. All of these songs still sound like they've just been recorded. That's how far ahead of the game these artists were.

Al Kooper was a member of Royal Teens ("Who Wears Short Shorts?") back in 1959. In 1966, he was a member of the Blues Project, whose music is just being rediscovered. In 1968, he became lead singer of Blood, Sweat and Tears. In 1969, he's on his own as an artist and producer with Columbia. We all know where BS&T is now. A new (and if I may opine, better) lead singer, David Clayton-Thomas, has really made this group. James Guercio, their producer now that Kooper is gone, is another reason for their success. You've got to know producers and their styles, too.

Choose your music by taste rather than charts. That means you've got to listen to all of it. Both sides of every single and album. If it's good, and if it fits, play it. That's the rule to go by. If it sells, that's fine. You're not there to sell records but to entertain your audience. If it doesn't sell and your audience begs for it, play it. Naturally you want to build a rapport with the record distributors so they'll keep you supplied with new material, but let them know the score. If you're not on a record, tell them. If they want you on it just because WWWW is on it, that's not a valid enough reason. If the record promo guy cites WNEW-FM in New York, WABX-FM in Detroit, KSAN-FM in San Francisco, or ABC-Love as being on the record then there is a basis for adding it to your show. However, that doesn't necessarily mean that it is suited for your particular audience, but it gives you something to go on.

The music you play must possess meaning and message. Make sure that it reflects contemporary attitudes. Make sure that it communicates with the audience you're trying to reach. Don't worry about who else is playing it in your market. If you break a record and the Top 40 picks it up, fine. That doesn't reduce the record's value to your audience. Many progressive stations have a tendency to drop records as soon as they are proven. This seems a little foolish to me. Consider it a pat on the back that you were so observant in your early response to the record.

As far as choosing music, you want all the best selling LP's in front of you, as well as the best selling singles. You've got to start somewhere, and this is a good place to start. To illustrate my point I'll use *Billboard*. There I've got the Hot 100 and Top LP's charts. I'll make note of the leading singles and albums and consider them for possible airplay.

Here's the key criterion: *No bubblegum or manufactured sounds!*

Let me give you a sample playlist from what's currently charted and my reaction to the entries:

SINGLES

1. "Aquarius/Let the Sunshine" by the Fifth Dimension.
   Yes! Make sure you play the long version. Very free, very meaningful sound for the "attitude" format.

2. "Hair" by the Cowsills.
   No! The Cowsills get a manufactured sound here that comes across as false compared to other material. Listen to it back to back with 5D and see. I played this in Atlanta in restricted time slots because of the unique situation there. We had only one Top 40 and no competition. Remember, all markets differ. Also get the Broadway cast LP of *Hair* and play these two songs and "Good Morning Starshine," "Where Do I Go," and "The Flesh Failures." The audience will appreciate it.

3. "It's Your Thing" by the Isley Brothers.
   Not often. It's got a complex arrangement that catches the trained ear, so it would be valid to play along with other blues pieces.

4. "Hawaii 5–0" by the Ventures.
   No! It was recorded for its commercial value only.

5. "You've Made Me So Very Happy" by BS&T.
   Yes! Yes! You should, however, give equal time to every cut on this album. There's rock, blues, and jazz on it. It's very inventive, very free, yet patterned enough to become a classic. These guys are very talented and very disciplined in their music.

6. "Time Is Tight" by Booker T.
   Sometimes. Booker T has become almost too slick. His style was funkier before "Hip Hugger." This would be a good piece for comparison. Play "Green Onions" and "Time Is Tight" back to back.

7. "Sweet Cherry Wine" by the Shondells.
   No! It's teeny-bopper material. You're not after this group unless they're ready for you.

8. "The Boxer" by Simon and Garfunkel.
   Yes! And this is about true for anything on their LP's. The other side of this single, "Baby Driver," is also excellent material.

9. "Atlantis" by Donovan.
   Yes! This song discusses, in the artist's usual poetic way, the story that holds fascination for many young adults. It poses the question "Was Atlantis important in our own evolution?" This song started in the underground in England, and it will probably always be heard on attitude stations.

10. "Get Back" by the Beatles.
    Yes! The Beatles are considered by most people to be the number one musical group in the world. Not rock, but musical. Their

material deserves much play and back-to-back comparison. Try some of the old backsides and obscure LP material that may never have hit the air. You know it sold. Did they ever have a flop album?

11. "Love Can Make You Happy" by Merci.
Not under ordinary circumstances because it smacks of teeny-bop-perism. Yet this record has that strange quality that makes us ask questions. The singing is flat as hell, but they're singing a valid line.

12. "Gimme, Gimme Good Lovin'" by Crazy Elephant.
No! As soon as you hear the rhythm track and see the names Kasenet and Katz, you know you've got bubblegum.

13. "These Eyes" by the Guess Who.
Yes! This is the type of record that "attitude" radio finds about two months before anyone else because it is listening to everything, including obscure Canadian masters.

14. "Only the Strong Survive" by Jerry Butler.
Sometimes. Jerry does a good reading of strong adult material.

15. "Chokin' Kind" by Joe Simon.
Same as with Jerry Butler. I would use these two artists in specific dayparts. For instance, my play in Atlanta held them to midday only. For most of the day, drop them.

16. "Do Your Thing" by the Watts Band.
No! This is simply noise with a beat. You want communication with words. You're after a message of some sort, remember? A live rock band can communicate by beat alone. You can't afford that in radio.

17. "Gitarzan" by Ray Stevens.
No!!

18. "Oh, Happy Day" by the Hawkins Singers.
Yes. Not often, mind you, but this started in the underground in San Francisco. Fine piece of music. Don't overreact by doing more gospel the way the record companies have.

19. "Galveston" by Glen Campbell.
No! He's gotten a little too slick and overproduced. Don't rule it out entirely if you want to make a thing about his TV show.

20. "I Don't Want Nobody to Give Me Nothin'" by James Brown.
Very seldom, as with other R&B things. With Otis Redding and Aretha Franklin you've got another story. They can do no wrong. But other R&B artists should be treated with care. Blues artists are in a different bag. Albert King is Blues, not R&B. B.B. King is Blues, not R&B. The same with Otis Bush. These people can and should be played.

ALBUMS

1. "Hair" Cast Recording.
Yes! Yes! Watch some of the cuts, because they get into questionable material. The beauty (and a damn shame as far as radio is concerned)

is that everything is said so well. All of the poor taste is handled in such an excellent way. Listen to it. All of it. See what you get from "Donna." See if the line "What a piece of work is man" in "Three-Five-Zero-Zero" rings a bell. Play "Aquarius," "Flesh Failures," "Hair," "Where Do I Go," "Good Morning Starshine," and maybe a couple of others. I doubt anyone else in town will play them.

2. "Blood, Sweat and Tears"
Yes! If you can find a bad cut, you win two weeks in West Virginia.

3. "Glen Campbell"
No!

4. "Donovan's Greatest Hits"
Sure. Get into "Season of the Witch" and "Catch the Wind," which are not U.S. superhits. Get his back LP's and program from as many of them as possible.

5. "Cloud Nine" by the Temptations.
Not on a regular basis.

6. "Nashville Skyline" by Bob Dylan.
Yes! Yes! We have a mandatory play at least every two hours at WPLO-FM. This is Dylan's most incredible LP. The duet with Johnny Cash will make your hair curl. All back Dylan LP's should be checked, especially his hits and all of the "John Wesley Harding" LP. Remember, the audience can't hear this anywhere else on radio.

7. "In A Gadda Da Vida" by Iron Butterfly.
Yes! The entire 17 minutes of the title cut should be played once a week or more. It's the best favor you can do for your audience. This heavy group can do no wrong.

8. "Tom Jones"
No! Manufactured. Too slick.

9. "Bayou Country" by Creedance Clearwater Revival.
Yes! This is good rock and roll. Note especially the long cuts. Bragging material there.

10. "Led Zeppelin"
Yes! They're an incredible blues group. Play the long cuts, which deserve to be heard. Lead guitarist, Jimmy Page, is a former Yardbird (like Eric Clapton and Jeff Beck), and he plays some mean licks here. Powerful.

11. "Englebert Humperdinck"
No!!

12. "Tom Jones Live"
Same as above. These guys are to the "attitude" format what Mike Douglas is to the Smothers Brothers.

13. "Ball" by Iron Butterfly.
Yes. Once again, this group can do no wrong. The cut "Soul Experience" is frightening in what it potentially can do to a seemingly stable mind.

14. "Birthday Party" by Steppenwolf.
    Yes. This group is one of the few valid hard rock groups, in that they play a basic 4/4 with no improvisation.

15. "Soulful" by Dionne Warwick.
    No!

16. "Fever Zone" by Tom Jones.
    No! Again, he is just not the right artist for this format. That's something you should tell the promo guys who try to get him played on your station.

17. "Association's Greatest Hits"
    Yes. But as oldies only.

18. "Funny Girl Soundtrack"
    No!!

19. "Switched On Bach"
    Yes. This is an electronic performance of J.S.B. Very effective, especially in our day of new computer technology.

20. "Romeo and Juliet Soundtrack"
    No! Don't laugh, though. Soundtracks can work. Cuts from "2001 Space Odyssey" and "Elvira Madigan" could be played.

The above is just to give you some idea where "attitude" radio is coming from. It is not a whole music list. I'd suggest programming like a Good Music station. That is, unlimited access to every cut in the library for use on the air at any time.

Here's the distinction and the beauty of the whole thing for us. You don't just play records. You can tell stories, trace the development of an artist, contrast and compare two or more versions of the same song. The trick is not to make a big thing out of it. No fanfare or rolling drums. With the toned down attitude, you don't stage things or really draw atttention to what you're doing, like they do elsewhere in radio—"Two In A Row!!"

You might just play Solomon Burke's "Proud Mary" and bump it at the end with Creedance's version. Don't say anything until the end. The audience knows what you're doing. Don't insult the listener's intelligence by, in essence, saying "Here's another record."

A few more ideas (and yours should be percolating, too, now that you have somewhat of a direction to follow):

CCR's "Good Golly Miss Molly" followed by Little Richard's original.

Donovan's first American hit, "Colours," followed by a middle period hit, like "Wear Your Love Like Heaven," the "Atlantis."

Any old Yardbirds hit followed by either Cream with Clapton or Beck or Page with Led Zeppelin. Try any other combination.

Subscribe to *Rolling Stone*. It follows rock from the inside. This will give you background, which you can use on the air to build segues. The production surrounding these segues should be kept simple. Drop jingles and stuff that clutters or gets in the way of the music.

Listen to as much material as possible. Find groups that are no longer together and use their material. Former groups like Buffalo Springfield, Cream, Traffic, Yardbirds, Sparrow, The Mugwumps, The Great Society, West Coast Pop Art Experimental Band, and the Spencer Davis Group. Delve into the more obscure, like Ars Nova, Velvet Underground, and New York Rock and Roll Ensemble.

In the folk idiom check out Buffy Sainte-Marie's "Now That the Buffalo Is Gone," an eloquent protest of Indian conditions. Her "Universal Soldier" is a good lament of the war. "Until It's Time For You to Go" and "Take My Hand For a While" are stirring love songs with a message.

Judy Collins' "I Think It's Going To Rain Today" describes man's inhumanity to man. She does a fine reading of Lennon and McCartney's "In My Life." "My Father" and "Someday Soon" are good also. When she does Leonard Cohen's "Suzanne," "Story of Isaac," and "Bird On the Wire" she's great, but then listen to Cohen's own renditions. Play Judy's "Albatross" or "Michael From the Mountains." The latter is a Joni Mitchell song, which only reminds me to tell you to listen to it too.

There are other folk artists that you should be studying, like Raun McKinnon and Janis Ian ("Janey's Blues" and "Mrs. McKenzie" tell us a lot about our environment). Listen to Joan Baez do Bob Dylan in "Any Day Now."

Don't ignore the mainstream groups in your quest of musical knowledge either. Check out the Rascals, the Beegees, The Who, even the Four Seasons, Beach Boys, and Grassroots. Hear the midroad people too, such as Jose Feliciano.

Examine them against those in our arena—the Beatles, Cream, Sly and Stone, MC5, Fudge, Bloomfield and Kooper (tap from "Supersession" more than from "Live Adventures"), Spirit, Blood, Sweat and Tears, Big Brother, Janis Joplin, Airplane, Steppenwolf, Jethro Tull, Ten Years After, John Mayall (look at back material with Bluesbreakers, too), Zombies, John Winter (Liberty has a better LP than Columbia, but play both), Hendrix, Stones, Rhinoceros, Traffic, and the Byrds (remember the Flying Burrito Brothers?).

There's so much material. So much great stuff. You'll find yourself trying to get it on the air. So stick with what you know until you get the hang of it. The audience will clue you in too.

There's one area that you should be particularly careful about—given the state of affairs with the FCC—and that's with lyrics. Listen to everything you plan to put on the air, and listen to every record until it ends. There's no sense jeopardizing the station's license, when we don't have to. Pay attention, too, for double entendre that may tend to cause a stir. If you have any doubts, talk it over with your manager. Play him the record, and let him call the shot. Usually the songs with "dirty" lyrics stick out like a sore thumb. Also worthy of note are those records with extremist political statements that may threaten the license and upset the community. The fact that other stations do it is not a good excuse to risk punitive actions. Let your good judgement prevail.

Keep your eye on trends in the industry, too. Right now, the Moog Synthesizer seems to be enjoying growing popularity. There's more and more computer music being pressed. You should know what's ahead so that you can exploit it for the benefit of your audience.

Some further thoughts:

Underground Overgrind: Too many of the so-called "underground" stations I've heard seem to overgrind their hard rock elements. They seem to aim at too narrow an audience. If it's the masses they reach, they must have cities full of quivering neurotics or so many people on grass that it may as well be stocked on the shelf with St. Joseph's Aspirin. It's my bet that these hardhardhard rock stations hurt themselves in the long run with audiences numbering 350 diehards. Several recent changes in the underground formula are proving me near right.

Dilute and Delight: What I'm trying to say is that I don't mind breaking tempo and pattern to balance the sound. It's not quite the "male/female/group/instrumental" mix that I learned at the Good Music station I once worked for, but you get the idea. Talking to my audience tells me that most who are nearing thirty years old are not fully sold on the electric and electronic stuff, although they like modern music. So they tolerate the hard material. Younger listeners wonder why I play a writer's version of a song. I do it because it is generally less strident.

Reference Preference: I like to use the word "reference." It means continuity or connectedness. It means consistency of attitude, which is another word I like to use. I use the word in reference to our music, because it seems to me that contemporary music is not necessarily "underground" or easily categorized as anything other than that—contemporary. The key requisite is that the material should express a modern "attitude" or reflect that attitude in people 18 to 30. Therefore, almost every piece of music to be played should have a reference to another piece of music. An example of what I'm trying to get across is Donovan's "Atlantis." The chord progression makes an obvious reference to the Beatles' "Hey Jude." The lyrics possess an obvious reference to "Those Were the Days" by Cream. Intentionally or not, use any of these references on the radio and it's a keen little set with, you might say, "attitude."

Citing Sets: Why simply play "Light My Fire" on the radio? I prefer to program "Light My Fire" on the radio. First Jools Driscol with Brian Auger. Then segue to Jose Feliciano, and climax with Jim Morrison.

There's an Atlanta group called the Arrangement. Folky. They put a Peter, Paul, and Mary sound to "Purple Haze." I play that, then Dion, then Hendrix.

But there are "references" other than just the same song by different artists' grouping. Try "Give Peace a Chance," followed by the "Ballad of John and Yoko," followed by "Crazy John," the Tom Paxton piece. How about "Signed D.C." by Love, "Codine" by Buffy or Quicksilver, "Amphetamine Angle" by Canned Heat, "The Pusher" by Steppenwolf? And on and on.

Bring on the Writers: I'm forever surprised to hear radio stations simultaneously claiming to be aware and excluding cuts from today's writers. Most of the material is downright great, because it pleases the ear and it also helps in the creation of sets. Rod McKuen is great for building female demographics (seems like all college-age women have a predilection for blond, besneakered poets). Song writers like Tom Paxton, Buffy Sainte-Marie, Raun McKinnon, Laura Nyro, and Janis Ian have so much to say. Then, of course, there's Dylan and Donovan and Donovan and Dylan . . .

No Shame, Not Shane: Oldies are interesting, to say the least. In some cases it's just the recall factor. A song is a catalyst to the past, and that can be good for the listener. "Ah, yes, I was with sexy Judy Martin back in 1961 when I first heard Ike and Tina Turner's 'Fool In Love' on the Stan Richards Show." But if that "moldy oldy memory maker from the stax of wax" is coupled with the new Ike and Tina material, we have real valid programming. Or if Jeff Beck's "Jailhouse Rock" is followed by Presley's version, hey, why not? It's texture and depth. How about "People Get Ready" by the Fudge and "People Get Ready" by the Temptations? Then there's the Phil Spector catalog then and now, the Beatles catalog then and now, the Stones catalog then and now . . .

Something Old: Thank God! Radio seems to have returned. The fact that a man can now go on the air and sound reasonably intelligent about his music, say what he has to say without insulting the listener's intelligence, and then get the hell out of the way and let the music do the talking gives me infinite joy. The on-air guy isn't reduced to blurting out clever things like "Hey, kiddoes, ain't that the grooviest tune you ever heard?" in order to retain the attention of the audience. With a subdued, non-announcerish delivery, he can relate as a real human being and get across more than all the catch phrases on the rest of the dial combined. It's an adult attitude that is conveyed in everything he does on the air. It is professional without being a robot about it.

Communicate with the audience. Unfortunately, some underground stations I've heard have confused the concept of relaxation and naturalness with sloppy, stuttering non-professionalism.

Something News: Music today can be so topical that many times it lends itself to use in newscast and public affairs features. Modern records can demonstrate a point or argue one, thereby better relating the news story or public affairs feature to the listener. Sadly, UPI and AP copy has no place in our kind of radio. It would be excellent if each newscast could be like "That Was The Week That Was."

Sell It Like It Is: When you really think about the business of radio, you realize that the commercials should be more entertaining than the music aired. After all, the music is played free. Some poor bastard has to pay for the commercial. A group of super-funny spots have begun to set a new pace nationally. That's encouraging, and we should take their lead. In our kind of radio, a spot has to be an exhilarating sixty second experience. It has to do more than in other formats.

NOTES

1. Tom Donahue, "Rotting Corpse," *Rolling Stone*, November 23, 1967, p. 14.
2. Julius Lester, foreword to Steve Post, *Playing in the FM Band* (New York: Viking, 1974), p. xiii.
3. Ben Fong-Torres, *San Francisco Chronicle*, May 20, 1993, P. E1.
4. Scoop Nisker, *If You Don't Like the News—Go Out and Make Some of Your Own* (Berkeley, CA: Ten Speed Press, 1994), pp. 52, 53.
5. Mike Gormley, "WABX Is David, Knocking 'Em Dead with Rock," *Detroit Free Press*, August 9, 1970, p. 6.
6. Jared Johnson, "WPLO-FM Is Versatile Station," *Atlanta Constitution*, May 17, 1969, p. 13.
7. "Commentary," *Metro Beat Magazine*, June 1969, p. 13.
8. Nisker, *If You Don't Like the News*, p. 50.
9. Karen Schoemer, "The Legacy of the Velvets," *New York Times*, December 3, 1989, p. H27.
10. Eric Rhoads, *Blast from the Past* (Boca Raton, FL: Streamline Press, 1996), p. 309.
11. Bruce Morrow, *Cousin Brucie: My Life in Rock and Roll Radio* (New York: Beech Tree Books, 1987), p. 176.
12. Rex Weiner, *Commentary*, 1972, p. 8.
13. Susan Krieger, *Hip Capitalism* (Hollywood: Sage Publications, 1979), p. 120.
14. Ibid., p. 167.
15. Richard Harringon, *Washington Post*, January 16, 1983, p. 28.

Chapter Four

Waist Deep in the Big Money

I do not believe the commercial per se is evil.
—Tom Donahue

Many commercial underground radio people felt uncomfortable with the entrepreneurial nature of their broadcast licenses. Counterculture activist Abbie Hoffman viewed these stations with a mixture of appreciation and suspicion. To him the jocks were cool enough, but the managers and owners were capitalist creeps. As one might suspect, his perspective was widely embraced by the former group and vociferously rebuked by the latter. Indeed, could a station legitimately claim to be underground when its raison d'être was ultimately the bottom line? As previously noted, certain social and cultural dissenters, like Eldridge Cleaver, scoffed at the notion, while others, such as drug guru Timothy Leary, embraced the idea, calling underground radio signals "cosmic vibecasts."

There was considerable dissension among station ranks on this point as well. Controversial deejay Roland Young, who was eventually fired for his outspokenness, stated on more than one occasion that nothing truly revolutionary could happen on the airwaves of a capitalist radio system—KSAN included.

To the left-leaning anti-establishment of the period, capitalists (including suburban parents, slumlords, scientists, and corporations who polluted the environment) were the despoilers and demons. They were the ravagers whose insatiable greed devoured all that was noble and good. Observed Theodore Roszak:

For a capitalist technocracy, profiteering will always be a central incentive and major corrupting influence. . . . The evils stem simply from the unrestricted pursuit of profit. Behind the manipulative deceptions there are capitalist desperados holding up the society for all the loot they can lay hands on.[1]

David Caute questioned the legitimacy of the counterculture, suggesting that one likely could not exist in such a zealously entrepreneurial environment, whose ultimate goal was the packaging and marketing of movements and trends for profit.

How counter was the counterculture in practice? Despite the punitive legislation introduced to check the use of drugs, the open, commercial societies of the West were able to accommodate outrageous gestures— and very often turn them to profit. In fact there was plenty of careerism and profit-taking within the counterculture itself.[2]

Russ Gibb: The profit motive was alive and well during counterculture times. I have yet to work at a radio station, or find one, including Pacifica outlets, where the bottom line was not money.

Dan Carlisle: There were always those who were suspicious of commercial undergrounds because they made money. I never thought the two were irreconcilable or totally incompatible. The whole thing wasn't about capitalism. It was about the social inequalities that existed.

Al Wilson: Well, I don't know. The commercial nature of these stations made it difficult to reconcile them with the counterculture message and image. It really depended on [from] what side of the fence you viewed the thing.

Thom O'Hair: I'm sure there were purists in the audience who felt that we sold out when we ran our first spot. These were the same people who thought that radio stations were owned by "rich guys," who had these stations to make money and get tax breaks. One time I was at a restaurant with a "purist" who was working for free at the local Pacifica station. He spent the entire evening going on and on about how much of a sellout KSAN was. At the end of the meal, he whipped out his dad's American Express Card to pay his half of the tab. That struck me as a perfect piece of punctuation to his sanctimonious diatribe.

Ed Shane: Some stations avoided any appearance of hypocrisy by refusing to use the term "underground." At WPLO we opted for "progressive rock." We used the term to disabuse those advertisers of the notion that "underground" meant Molotov cocktail–wielding longhairs who burned Bank of America branches and supplied their daughters with cheap drugs.

Thom O'Hair: I believe a lot of the criticism about "selling out" stemmed from the fact that FM itself had always been viewed as a sort of public service option or alternative to the money-making AM band. In fact, FM had been a nonfactor in the sale of airtime, so when it began to sell, some people reacted in a negative way.

Al Wilson: Maybe it was idealistic to think the combination would work. However, the selling of commercials made the underground approach possible.

Allen Shaw: I'd have to agree. I believe that most major change or creative innovation in broadcast media is the result of pure creativity meeting commercial potential. Without commercial potential, programming will not survive for very long, unless it is directly subsidized by institutions, listeners, or tax dollars. Broadcasting in America is an extension of the free enterprise system. Profit is always the ultimate objective. Those who feel that this is bad need only listen to radio services in Canada, Britain, or the former Soviet bloc countries to hear what a quasi–free enterprise system has to offer its audience. Commercial underground radio happened in this country because it was fortunate enough to be attempted in this country. Our system of radio is totally driven by the public's interest in certain programming forms. What could be more democratic? Therefore, to be commercial and underground is not diametrical. This country has produced the most diverse presentation of radio product in the world. It was in this context that freeform commercial underground radio was born, lived, and died. The concept grew out of rebellion against established structures of Top 40 radio. It was a reflection of a new brand of rock music and a generation that espoused a whole new value system, which was very different from prior generations. During the socially and culturally charged period of 1967 through the early 1970s, commercial underground radio was attractive to a large enough segment of the population to have real commercial appeal. A unique convergence involving hippies, civil rights activists, antiwar protesters, anti-establishment rebels, coming of age baby boomers, new progressive rock scene, stereophonic equipment, and hungry FM station owners made this kind of radio possible.

Ed Shane: Napoleon called the British "a nation of shopkeepers," and that heritage was passed down to Britain's emancipated American colonies. The U.S. was founded on commerce. Advertising is the outgrowth of American business' need to inform the public of its wares. Underground radio emerged in the context of pure American commercialism, but with a keen sensitivity about hype and the crassness of overcommercialism. Stations run by universities and foundations (like Pacifica) were the exceptions, not the rule. Most of the early commercial underground outlets were operated by broadcast companies that were in business to make a profit. The great irony of the commercial underground format is the support it received from major operators like Plough and Metromedia.

Dan Carlisle: If agents of change are rebels, then these stations were revolutionary in their very own unique way. We believed that our kind of innovative radio could really say something, break new ground, and, yes, make money. That's a rather revolutionary notion unto itself.

Larry Miller: We were revolutionary in every sense of the word, yet we were driven by commercial motives. The socialist revolution hadn't happened. We were, in fact, living in a capitalist society, so making money was a natural event. Some very naive political types thought everything should be free, but they hadn't explained that to our landlords, the grocery store, or the utility companies, so we had no choice but to embrace, however dubiously or gingerly, mammon. We weren't greedy, but we weren't stupid either. Only a handful of politically correct folks decided it was unworkable and bailed out. When we first went on the air with the format at KMPX and WABX, we were mistakenly perceived as noncommercial because we had no spots yet. As we became more successful and began to run some, we were charged by the ignorant with selling out. In the long run, it didn't make any real difference, because they listened to us anyway. We had the only game in town initially, and the commercials were as hip as the music. Hey, what the hell, deejays need to eat, too. The main reason these stations were commercial was that the existing noncommercial stations at the time were too snobbish to consider playing something as "pop" as rock music. These college/public/educational outlets played "adult" stuff, but never rock. The irony of that was that the flavor of commercial FM alternative rock programming was inspired by the noncom, Pacifica type station.

WATERBED RADIO

The hippies were becoming a substantial marketing demographic.
—Scoop Nisker

Mainstream advertisers were not the clientele of early underground outlets, and for good reason, noted *Advertising Age,* as it assessed the changing nature of the listening public:

> Marketing's traditional demographic measurement yardstick will now have to be supplemented with studies of the new attitudes that are developing in our society toward possessions, fashions, quality of life and advertising. Demographic measurements seldom measure social change—yet social innovation, for the next decade or two, will compel greater marketing innovations.[3]

Dwight Douglas: These innovations were slow to benefit the first underground stations. FM certainly did have to establish itself with the "lifestyle" advertiser, like waterbed stores, head shops, concert promoters, and record outlets. Fifty percent of all advertising came from the record companies either directly or through cooperative buys with local promoters and store owners.

Tim Powell: There was, I think, an honesty to these stations that made "commercial" success limited to the services, products, and establishments that fit this image. If anyone thinks for a moment that the national sponsors were lining up to get on the early FM stations, they're screwy. At least it did not happen out west, perhaps on the East Coast. For big markets, these stations were run like candy stores. Tradeouts for furniture for the station owner, trades for cars for the general manager, those were the things that were happening on the larger account level.

Roland Jacopetti: At one point, KSAN was trying to sell the Bank of America on an ad campaign. The bank actually consented to meet with station reps, so a bunch of people went to their advertising offices in downtown San Francisco. Among those who went was our talk show guy, Travis T. Hipp. The bank was very touchy about its image in the hip world, particularly as this was just a few weeks after their branch in Vista, California, had been pelted with rocks and finally burnt to the ground. Travis thought, under the circumstances, we could construct an excellent campaign around the slogan "There's a Bank of America a stone's throw from where you live." I believe the meeting ended soon after he made that suggestion.

Tim Powell: As I recall, the Bank of America finally did get on, and it didn't make some of us very happy either, since it was the target of a great deal of counterculture animosity. In those days, B of A's were the target of almost every demonstration, and many branches had been attacked, so this was a problem for the station. On top of everything else, the bank really wanted on at any cost, so this forced the issue, and on they were. To mitigate their presence on our station, we got them to agree to a tag line that might put their spot in a better context for us. We took the big cash from the Antichrist, and our listeners got a laugh at the "stone's throw" reference. We were able to sleep with the devil and pull his tail at the same time.

Larry Miller: From the start our listeners were perceived as using products, goods, and services that were unique to them—records, waterbeds, clothing, dope paraphernalia, posters, and so forth. Items for hippies. Our listeners were also perceived as using the same products as everyone else. They wore Levis, drank Coke, and drove VWs. By 1970, many ad agencies were doing spots especially for the underground/progressive FM station. As early as 1968, Jefferson Airplane did some Levi spots, which resulted in it being accused by the undergound press as having sold out. It was a ticklish time.

During the first couple of years of its existence, the underground station could claim dominance in one area of advertiser support—the waterbed store. For example, Raechel Donahue estimates that at one point, KSAN

Radio Atlanta

FM Rate Card No. 5
(Effective May 1, 1970)

PLOUGH BROADCASTING COMPANY, INC.

805 Peachtree St., NE, Atlanta, Ga. 30308   Telephone: 404-872-5851

Represented Nationally by: HR Representatives, Inc.

ANNOUNCEMENTS

One minute, rotating—Live or transcribed

I MINUTE	"AAA" (7 p.m.-12 mid.)	"AA" (3-7 p.m.)	"A" (6 a.m-3 p.m.)
I Time	$18.00	$17.00	$15.00
52 Times	17.00	16.00	14.00
104 Times	16.00	15.00	13.00
156 Times	15.00	14.00	12.00
260 Times	14.00	13.00	11.00
312 Times	13.00	12.00	10.00
364 Times	12.00	11.00	9.00
520 Times	11.00	10.00	8.00
1040 Times	10.00	9.00	7.00

30 Seconds = 80% of Minute Rate

SATURATION PACKAGES
(One Minute)

TIMES	"AAA"	"AA"	"A"
6	$102.00	$ 96.00	$ 84.00
12	192.00	180.00	156.00
18	270.00	252.00	216.00
24	336.00	312.00	264.00
36	468.00	432.00	360.00
48	576.00	528.00	432.00

TOTAL AUDIENCE PLAN

TIMES	"AAA"	"AA"	"A"	WEEKLY
6	2	2	2	$ 90.00
12	4	4	4	168.00
18	6	6	6	234.00
24	8	8	8	288.00
36	12	12	12	396.00
48	16	16	16	480.00

ROS—SUNDAY—SATURDAY
(Best time available)

10 Per Week—$13.00   25 Per Week—$12.00   50 Per Week—$10.00

Time is money at WPLO-FM.

had almost every Bay Area waterbed account on the air, which was over a half dozen.

> *Raechel Donahue:* Within months most were out of business because of the stiffness of the competition. I remember someone observing that our listeners must spend a lot of time smokin' and floatin', or bongin' and ballin'.

BITING THE HAND . . .

> They call virtue their ungratefulness.
>
> —Philip Sidney

At any commercial station, regardless of the type of programming it broadcasts, the objective of the sales department is to get advertisers to buy airtime. There is nothing vague about its mission or mandate. Plainly and simply speaking, it is to sell as many spots and/or sponsorships to local and national businesses as possible, and this was no less true for underground stations. This fact, however, was a common source of conflict between what turned out to be two disparate and ultimately adversarial groups in this type of radio. Programming and sales were from Venus and Mars, respectively.

> *Kate Ingram:* This stemmed from the fact that the air staffs usually were a more idealistic breed than the sales staffs. This resulted in misunderstanding between the programming side and the sales and ownership end.

> *Stefan Ponek:* This created constant and ongoing tension at the station. While we liked the sales guys, because we demanded they be counterculture too, we made their job extremely difficult. The earliest sales reps were long-haired and strangely dressed, and we printed them business cards in psychedelic lettering on 3 by 5 stock. It just didn't fit the regular card file, and that was the whole idea. We worked hard to make these kinds of statements. Our station poster was by Mouse and Kelly, rock artists at the time. Sales presentation materials featured this artwork and other artifacts of the culture. Rick Griffin did one. We shunned the Peter Max "flowers-in-the-hair, love image," and held to a kind of purity of taste, which frustrated the advertising community and probably some of our sales people as well. Whether we did this to get the satisfaction that comes from constantly staying one up, I couldn't say

exactly. I think we genuinely believed in our feeling for the rightness of everything. It was based in a shared LSD experience that the commercial world just didn't "get."

Thom O'Hair: For many of the jocks the sales people were the villains. This was an individual whose moral code existed in the murky shadow of his greed. This person would allow anything to happen for money. No tale of corruption and evil left out the sales guy when programming people got together to talk in the staff lounge. Sales reps were rat bastards with money-grubbing ways, and every time they'd bring in a spot schedule, they were given grief— "They're not right for our kind of station," "They're owned by XYZ Corporation that kills babies," "They produce material for the Vietnam War machine." . . . We had a million objections, and this obviously generated hostilities.

Russ Gibb: We got a little out there on this, and the owner would have to intervene to keep us from ruining the commercial value of the station.

John Gehron: Stations often had to be reclaimed by the owners, especially in light of the fact that revenues were being sacrificed. When this took place, as you can image, things really got tense and there was an outpouring of criticism from the air staff, which objected to such "capitalistic" interference.

Dan Carlisle: The jerks who ran a lot of these stations, like KWEST, KSHE, and WABX—Century Broadcasting—were real tyrants when it came to a buck. They were devoid of humanity. I mean these jokers hated people and treated them deplorably. They were crooks, and that's about the best thing that can be said about them.

Lee Abrams: The owners of many of these stations tended to be pure capitalists, frequently masquerading as saviors.

Tim Powell: This contempt for management carried over to the sponsor as well. Once a station I was working at got a Coke buy, and there [were] explicit agency instructions about the schedule posted on the production studio wall. Someone converted the "C" in Coke to a cent sign and the "S" in schedule to a dollar sign. The general manager (who I'm told was a speed freak) went ballistic and accused me of defacing the instruction sheet. This guy claimed I was anti-commercial radio, or something to that effect, although I'd been working my ass off in production. When he told one of his old Top 40 buddies at the station about the incident, the guy admitted that it had been his pen that had, in fact, perpetrated the crime. In his defense, he told the manager he'd done this simply to point out that the station was finally making some dough. This pleased the boss but did not win me any points.

Roland Jacopetti: I think the thing the air staff feared the most was overcommercialization. There was a lot of campaigning against too many ads and ads that didn't fit what we were trying to do, but there was also a feeling that the power was not entirely in the hands of the suits. Our creativity and skill still gave us a certain amount of power. We could make suggestions and even demands because they knew we were doing a good job. There has always been warfare between programming and sales departments in radio, and not just underground radio, although it experienced more than its share.

Shelley Grafman: When all the noble posturing was done, the fact of the matter was that you had to survive, and that meant airing advertisements. As managers, we tried to strike a balance between these two points of view, or factions, if you will. But in the end, it took revenue to keep these people and what they were doing and saying on the air.

Thom O'Hair: It's unfortunate, but hardly anybody gave any credit to the sales people for keeping the stations afloat. In many ways, that would have to be the untold story of underground radio. Were it not for the guys who got out there and faced a tough sell, we wouldn't be talking about this right now. It was a hell of a job to get this FM thing across to prospective advertisers. Uphill all the way.

Larry Miller: Well, when all is said and done, you can't eat ideals. No commercials also meant very small paychecks and sometimes none at all. My first gig at KMPX was a six-hour airshift each night. My hourly wage was $1.50, or $42.50 a week. When the advertising finally began coming in, at least I could pay my rent, because my salary was able to be raised.

OUT, DAMNED SPOTS!

Less music and more commercials on the Magic Bus . . .

If the airing of commercials was considered an inevitable evil—something that programmers simply had to live with—then, at least, intense scrutiny could and would be levied upon the content of these unwelcome little violators of the underground radio aesthetic. Peter Fornatale and Joshua Mills observed that "the on-the-air personnel at progressive stations often treated their medium as a personal political platform, a tool in a social movement—and only secondarily a business."[4]

Dwight Douglas: A station's sociopolitical philosophy invariably entered into how commercials were viewed and treated.

Ben Fong-Torres: The revolutionary zeal of these stations engendered the basic aversion to the commercial, or certainly the commercial sound.

Lee Abrams: The general idea was to avoid appearing commercial. The image was revolutionary. That was the goal anyway. I believe most of the staff members considered themselves "rebels," so you could expect a negative reaction to airing spots.

Shelley Grafman: KSHE was always sensitive to commercial content and on numerous occasions refused prepared tapes because they possessed offensive text.

Roland Jacopetti: During my initial tenure at KSAN, the station was undergoing its first burst of popularity. We were beginning to get the automatic national buys based on our decent Arbitron ratings. Everyone hated this except the sales department. One evening I was carting up a series of commercials from a clothing store chain. It was a super-corny campaign, couched in a pseudo answer-man format. All the spots went something like this:

Voice I: Dear (Store) Answer Man, My brilliant son has decided he wants to go and work with Indians. I told him if he does that, no one will ever see him again. Who ever heard of anyone making a name for himself working with Indians? (Signed) Agonized.

Voice 2: Dear Agonized, Haven't you ever heard of General Custer?

Well, I shut the tape off and bolted into the GM's (Willis Duff) office and said, "Willis, I've finally hit a national commercial that, if you want it put on cart, you'll have to do it yourself!" With that, he asked to hear it and we headed back to the production room where I played it for him. "You're right," he said. "It is objectionable." He called the agency who'd sent the tape to us and they agreed to his suggestion that the "Indian" spot be dropped from the overall rotation. A week or so later, the account exec at the agency called and informed us that out of 189 stations running the campaign, we were the only one that complained about the Indian spot. He then insisted that it be returned to rotation. Willis, God bless him, said, "Then we don't want your business," and we lost the account.

Ben Fong-Torres: I remember a time at the station when the U.S. Army wanted to get on the air, but there was strong opposition to it, so it didn't happen.

Dusty Street: It was a philosophical thing. It would have been hypocritical of us to allow Army on or Standard Oil, especially after they had polluted the Bay Area with an oil spill. If we did run a Pepsi spot, we wanted to run our own version, not the garbage sent to us from Madison Avenue. We created something that would be directly tuned into our audience. When this latitude was eventually taken away from us, the gig was up for underground/freeform stations.

Ed Shane: Most of us established stringent rules about commercials. At WPLO, for example, content, product, presentation style, and copy had to conform to the overall concept of the station. We rejected some of the national ads because of the political aspects of their products. I should add that because the station was new at its format and had very little recognition at the national advertising level, we didn't have to worry much. Most of our commercials were local and lifestyle-oriented. There was certainly no anxiety on management's part when we rejected a commercial, because we were getting advertisers the station never had before. The only complaints I heard when I rejected an ad or a campaign [were] from the station account executive whose commission depended on clearance.

Allen Shaw: During this whole era, many of these stations, including the ABC-FM stations, adopted a policy governing what kind of commercials could be aired. The deejays were usually the censors. In a kind of communal fashion, commercials were played in jock staff meetings. If the commercial was for a bank or a chemical company, or an auto manufacturer (especially General Motors), it was sure to be rejected. An ad agency commercial that was too slickly produced, a jingle, or a traditional deep-voiced announcer would also be rejected. After a pleading from the general manager that the station needed the revenue to pay the deejays that month, permission would be given to air the spot if it were re-recorded in a style considered appropriate for the station's sound and psyche. Thus, slick agency copy for Pioneer Stereo, for instance, would be scrubbed in favor of a live deejay ad libbing from notes about the product. In 1969, WABX in Detroit actually made an agency recording for pHisohex acne treatment counterculture-friendly by beeping over the word "pimple" whenever it appeared in the commercial.

Dan Carlisle: One of my favorite examples of a new approach to commercials was also from WABX. Stanley Cohen, a local Detroit hippie biz' man, owned a hip shoe store called the "Just Looking Bootery." He was savvy enough to instruct me and Dave Dixon to do whatever we wanted as long as we got the address correct. The commercial we made for one of Stan's all too frequent sales events started with Dave extolling the virtues of the product line of platform shoes while occasionally admonishing Stan for his lapses in taste concerning his stock. The commercial ended with the location and name of the store, followed by the sound of calliope music and my voice over it saying, "Don't forget to ask for your free slap in the face." Music out.

Roland Jacopetti: To kind of make the whole commercial thing less of a turnoff for us and our audience, we came up with a sort of antidote. Still bugged by the number of corny national spots, I asked Willis if we could make some "anti" spots, which would utilize the format of the objectionable spot and lampoon it in some fashion. I said, "We can instruct the jocks never to play an anti-spot back to back with the commercial being satirized." Willis must have been distracted because he agreed. I remember[ed] a local comedy group's work (the Congress of Wonders), and I made a very funny anti-Vitalis spot about "My Phallus" hair tonic. Then we got a series of spots from Evelyn Wood Reading Dynamics, a speed-reading course, featuring very stilted student voices saying, "Hi. I learned to read three thousand words a minute at Evelyn Wood." I took these testimonials, chopped them up, and inserted phrases from them in wild skits I made up. The jocks loved them. Then I guess one of the jocks played one of these back to back with a real Evelyn Wood spot while they were tuned in, and the shit hit the proverbial fan. The client called and threatened everything from killing the schedule to legal action to bodily harm. Willis called me and asked what the hell I was doing, and I reminded him that he'd given his blessing. He just shook his head quizzically and said, "I did?"

Ed Shane: Not all spots received a satirical treatment, but most were certainly written to reflect who we were and what we were about. Here's a relatively routine example of this approach for an account called "Sexy Sadie" that ran on WPLO-FM:

Twas the night before Christmas and down on the strip there were persons just buying their clothes to look hip. Bird sellers were out on the street with their hawkings. Some folks were rapping and others just talking. Street children were nestled all snug in their beds, while visions of coloring danced in their heads. When atop Sexy Sadie there arose such a clatter that street freaks and straights tried to find a long ladder. Scramble to the roof said the shoppers inside. There must be more clothing they're trying to hide. And once they were up there, what did they find but a fat little man with a padded behind. His eyes how they rolled. His dimples how merry. His little red suit made him look like a fairy. He had an odd pipe and held it ever so stiff, while federal agents crept up for a sniff. Holly leaves they'd allow and leave with chagrin, and the old man laughed and pulled at his chin. To the crowd that had gathered he addressed man and lady. "Please buy your presents down at Sexy Sadie's. 1010 Peachtree. Your mistletoe smoking headquarters."

PRODUCTION VALUES

Anaximenes called it air.

—Robert M. Pirsig

Most radio stations back in the 1960s (as today) discussed production values as they pertained to the efficacy of a mix in spots or music cuts or segments. At underground outlets, the word "values" possessed a double connotation, which carried it far beyond its standard application at other commercial stations.

In a 1970 magazine interview that noted the distinctive manner in which commercials were put together at underground operations, Chicago radio program director Thom Trunnell remarked that his production team sought to create the "non-commercial commercial."

> [We] try to . . . produce commercials that don't offend, that . . . are true examples of honesty in writing and delivery. . . . As long as commercials must be broadcast in the context of the programming, why not make them as honest as possible in this concept, and match your programming?[5]

Roland Jacopetti: Noncommercial commercial might be a good way to describe the sound we were after. During the time I was a maker of radio spots in this programming genre, I was always conscious of the need to be nonassaultive. I remember when Edward Bear was the all-night man on KSAN. He had a few ads on his show, and every so often there'd be something that was irritating or raucous. Bear, knowing that many of his wee-hour listeners were screwing or tripping, would prepare for these spots well in advance by slowly increasing the tempo and energy of the music he was playing so as not to jolt his audience. This was really all he could do on these occasions. Consideration for the listener, and a feeling of kinship with the audience, strikes me as one of the hallmarks of underground rock stations.

Stefan Ponek: High-intensity mixes were the exception. Our style was definitely a reaction to what was perceived by all of us as too much hype in radio presentation. In the early years, we resisted agency-produced commercials with inappropriate mixes. It was a big concession when the first Coke jingle finally got on the air. We considered our style to be ultra laid-back, but it was caricatured by our critics who mocked the long "stony" pauses and ethereal sounds in spots.

Thom O'Hair: We'd remix outside spots as much as possible to retain our aura. Once we got a big buy for this mouthwash, some crap you sprayed in your mouth. It consisted of a jingle, a big voice, and a lot of compression, so we redid it. Our replacement used a track by Cream called "Fresh Garbage" as a bed. Anyway, the Cleos are announced—they're like the Academy Awards of radio commercials—and our damn version was nominated. I don't recall it winning, but here's the rub. The ad agency that had produced the original spot, the one we shit-canned, thought they were the winners and got all excited. Then they found out that it was the KSAN replacement spot that was up for the prize—doom and gloom. The fecal matter really hit the swirling blades. Lawyers wrote letters and filed papers. Metromedia had to provide "make-goods" at about five to one, and that forced us to put the dreck spot on the air and many more times than originally scheduled. All we could do was grin and bear it, and run the spots very low. We used to under-modulate as plan "B." If we got a bad spot and couldn't redo it, we'd just peak the V.U. meter to 30 percent and it would kind of fade away. One of the unfortunate by-products of increased ratings was that the rates would go up and this would push out local advertisers who didn't have the budgets of the nationals. The loyal local advertiser found it harder and harder to afford us as we grew in audience size. Unfortunately, local advertisers were the best for the station in a couple of important ways. First the production department did the mixing. The production department at KSAN was exceptional. Roland Jacopetti and Rick Sadle did the production while I was there. Jacopetti was there before Sadle. These guys could make a spot selling shit sound great. The commercials had a very KSAN-like feel all the time. This made the station sound great. Believe it or not, we would get requests for certain spots. That's how damn good they were. The national spots were a different story. They were donut jingled with heavy "AM-voiced" announcers. A ton of compression was another element that made them suck. We were an evolving radio format, and we had to air that primal slime. Often the production people would use the same national copy but put their own unique stamp on the production part. We got away with this until the Cleo Awards caper.

The same experience was common in the format around the country. Underground stations sought to keep the integrity of their sound intact, even if it meant coming to blows with deep-pocketed sponsors. Simply put, the production values in commercials, local or national in nature, had to fit the "nonformat" format. "A lot of very large companies have wanted to go on 'ABX but refuse to alter their presentation from the AM style. They aren't on the station," noted radio columnist Mike Gormley.[6]

When it came to dealing with commercials, underground stations even treated their scheduling differently. To begin with, the number of spots allowed per hour was typically half that on Top 40 stations. Their placement during the hour was novel as well.

> *Raechel Donahue:* Even our approach to logging commercials was different. Top 40 alternated singles songs and single commercials. We decided to play both songs and commercials in groups of three. Tom told the salesmen they couldn't sell thirty-second spots because when people heard commercials they just heard spots; they didn't recognize whether they were a sixty or a thirty. When the sales guys protested, he told them they could sell thirties but at the same rate as the sixties. That got the point across, and half-minute commercials were gone.

One of the format's bragging rights had to do with audience and advertiser loyalty. It was widely known on the street and in the boardrooms that the underground oeuvre was a tight one, a point that sales people were sure to note in their presentations to prospective clients.

> *Dwight Douglas:* The underground advertiser was very loyal and seldom wandered too far. Of course, the old "birds of a feather" phrase has some applicability here.

> *Roland Jacopetti:* In this format, listeners really listened and responded to sponsor messages. The audience went to their stores and bought their products. KSAN listeners really did tend to be loyal to KSAN advertisers, and I've never known advertisers to take a more active interest in what was on the air for them. It was a full and satisfying relationship in that respect.

PACKAGING LOVE

Love is another name for God!

—Peter Tork

Carla Brooks Johnston: Packaging love became the way to unify those fractured by the poverty, discrimination, war, disrespect from parents—the WWII generation who simply wanted proper unquestioning conformity. Packaging love became the alternative for those who knew that the God of their childhood was certainly dead. Music was the only outlet for all these feelings. The flower children needed a new reality.

Excerpts from a series of what were confidential corporate memos (dated November 4, 11, and 18, 1968) relating to ABC's "Love" format are presented below. The format was on the cusp of its debut, and the network's sales, promotion, and programming departments were gearing up.

THE SIXTH DEFINITION OF LOVE (NOVEMBER 4)

Webster's lists five definitions of the word "love." Love is the overall name for our new programming too. We hope to become so popular that our radio stations are thought of as a sixth definition or, at the very least, that they are associated with the word—love. . . .

Our Love will be a reflection of the new music and thinking. We'll be in the progressive rock bag, but the music is only an indicator of a more deeply rooted set of changes in our society. In the ten months we've been developing this programming, hopefully we've not only learned to select the right music, but also to add the humor and content that form the new social change. . . .

When we say Love, we imply no sensuality. Rather, we're talking about the new feeling of brotherhood and understanding among all peoples. Love is black and white, old and young, rich and poor, father and son, boy and girl, and country and nation. . . .

It will be very important to create the proper, unified, image of our Love in each market. We will be known on the air simply as Love—not "love radio" or "the sound of love"—just plain Love. . . .

The primary on-air voice of the program service is that of John Rydgren, who will be known simply as Brother John. . . .

When will we be going on the air? As soon as possible from your end and our end. Except for WLS, all of our stations will be airing the new programming via automation. . . .

WABX-FM station logo.

STONES/BEATLES MONTH IN HOLDING PATTERN

Our original idea was to produce special, promotional tapes containing nothing but Beatles and Rolling Stones records—songs by the two top groups. This would be aired for about a month prior to the new Love programming kick-off. There would be no off-air promotion. It would simply be a dramatic, on-air marathon indicating that something new is happening on our FM. Promos for Love would be run between the Beatles and Stones disks. This would also serve as a trial period for the new automation system to make sure everything works perfectly. . . .

Stones/Beatles month is now in a holding pattern for a couple of reasons. You are probably aware of John Lennon's double problems: an arrest for possession of marijuana and the refusal of EMI to distribute an album featuring a full, frontal nude of himself and his girlfriend. Needless to say, this kind of publicity could make us come off in the wrong light. Let us note, however, that there have been no reports of any station dropping the Beatles' hit ("Hey Jude") because of this publicity. Stations continued playing Rolling Stones' records when they too were involved in pot charges. . . .

But there is another reason for this holding pattern. Both the Beatles and Stones have a new album due for imminent release. If we do the Beatles/Stones thing at all, we'd like to include the new album cuts for added punch. The allegedly dirty album cover for the new Stones' LP has been scrapped. The new Beatles' album is not the one with the proposed nude picture. The nude cover is for Lennon's own LP venture. . . .

As of today, Beatles/Stones month is neither on nor off. We're just waiting to see what happens. By [and] large, the negative publicity surrounding the album covers and pot charge has subsided. It should be completely gone by the forthcoming release of "Yellow Submarine," the Beatles' animated feature film, which has received critical raves. . . .

WHO'S ON FIRST

The decision to go ahead with Stones/Beatles month or to drop it will be made at the last minute. At that time, we'll weigh all the factors and do one of three things: 1. Go ahead with Beatles/Stones month—about 15 one hour-long tapes to be repeated; 2. Start right off with the Love format, eliminating any on-air promotional tease; or 3. Produce about 15 hours of progressive rock music tapes (not the Love format) to be used as an on-air promotion until the actual Love programming begins. . . .

Why should we do 3 instead of 1 or 2? This plan will be used only if the stations are ready to carry tapes before our studio and duplicating equipment are completed. We are now capable of turning out either a simple Beatles/Stones or progressive rock music format, but we are not yet equipped to produce our complicated Love format and to duplicate the 25 one hour-long tapes, which will be sent to each station weekly. . . .

In short, what goes on and when will be determined as soon as one or two stations are ready to roll. Each of the six may begin at different times, and each may not begin with the same programming. Time will tell. . . .

FLACKMAN '69

The six week promotional kick-off for Love will most probably cover the last three weeks in January and the first three weeks in February. There's no sense in bucking the holidays with our hoopla. Delaying the kick-off campaign will also allow us to make sure the programming and automation are functioning with no hitches. It'd be just great to create interest and have a lot of people tune in to hear Jimi Hendrix accompany the latest news from the American FM Network. . . .

George Yahraes is creating a package of promotional ideas, items and sources from which each station's promotion director can draw. Special news release forms, glossies of Brother John, the Love logo in umpteen different varieties, press release information, ad layouts, and a record store poster are in the works. . . .

A MAP IS IN THE BAG

We are working cooperatively with a leading publisher to produce a monthly Love magazine to be distributed in each of our markets. The 68 pager would feature 14 pages of full-color and would be printed on slick stock. Hopefully tagged "Love" (there may be a legal hang up here), the magazine would reflect in print what we will be about on the air. Editorially the magazine will zero in on progressive rock groups and the new social thinking. Although a great deal of space would be devoted to us (including station call letters), we would have no financial obligation. The publisher would give us the space and use our logo on the front cover in return for spots promoting the magazine. . . .

If the publisher finds publication of a special magazine for us too costly, we will most definitely try to tie in with "Eye" magazine on a trade out basis—at least one page per month for an ad and maybe a column by Brother John. We'll keep you up to date on the progress of our publishing tie-in. . . .

THE LEFT AND RIGHT CHANNEL

A key point in our promotional effort will be the fact that we're stereo. Among our plans are an extensive on-air campaign promoting

stereo in a unique and humorous manner. We are exploring the possibility of cooperating with other FM stations (market by market, as well
as nationally) to push consumer purchase of FM stereo receivers for
home, car, and portable use. . . .

More on this stereo promo later. For now, we suggest you enroll your
station in the ranks of the NAFMB (National Association of FM
Broadcasters), if you have not already done so. NAFMB should prove
most helpful to us individually and collectively—for the stereo campaign and other efforts too. . . .

BLACK INK IS BEAUTIFUL

The Love programming is targeting the college audience, but hopes
to catch both older and younger age groups who think much as the
college student does about progressive rock, social change, and love.
We may well find ourselves going after a group of people who think
and feel the same way, rather than a specific age or income group.
Our programming is designed to appeal to a person with a certain set
of emotional and intellectual characteristics—whether he is 17 or
38. . . .

The sales approach, rates, and national representation of all our FM
stations for group buys present some sticky situations. In a recent memo
to station and sales managers, George Yahraes presented some possible
approaches for consideration and discussion. Within the next few
weeks, Hal and George will be talking to all station and sales managers
in an effort to come up with as unified a sales approach as possible that
still allows for individual market situations. . . .

Whether we try some new ideas or stick with proven plans, the desire
is to prove that black ink is beautiful—especially with FM. . . .

THE NUMBERS GAME

A regular feature of the Love format will be the American Dialogue
line where listeners call in to a special local number and record their
views. Tapes from each station will then be sent to New York for editing
and inclusion in the master tapes. Thus Love will present a cross section
of new thinking from all parts of the country. . . .

To effect this locally, each station will need to install an automatic
recording device that will allow Brother John to offer a station-custom-
ized greeting and permit the caller to sound-off for as long as he likes.
In addition to the recorder, an easily remembered phone number will
determine the success of the American Dialogue line in your market.
Why not start checking with the phone company now for a number like
"L-O-V-E-9-5-5," "A-B-C-L-O-V-E," and the like.

❖ ❖ ❖

AN APPLE A DAY (NOVEMBER 11)

The Beatles' company, Apple Corps, is preparing a speculative jingle tape for us. We contacted Apple several months ago to see if they would be interested in such a venture. After listening to a Love audition tape and reading our programming philosophy, they decided to give it a try. . . .

We heard nothing for quite a while, but the latest from London is that the jingles are being worked on. With the Beatles' many other activities, progress may be slow. A capella jingles from PAMS will get us started with the Apples' jingles to be added as soon as available. . . .

Creatively, the Apple ideas should be right in our bag, although there may be a "cost gap" to bridge. Let's hope we can get Apple jingles on the air and soon. The on and off the air publicity value will be fantastic. . . .

FIVE A DAY

Each station will be receiving 25 fresh tapes weekly. But instead of changing all the tapes at one time, the replacement will be at the rate of five hours per day. This way a new release or current event can be aired within 24 hours—making us almost as up to date as if we were live. . . .

REAL REELS

Station managers will soon be receiving a presentation and demonstration tape of the Love programming. These should give all concerned a fairly accurate idea of what the actual service will be in terms of content and breaks. We're still tooling up (carting album cuts, producing thematic segments, etc.) and waiting for the final pieces of equipment. Thus, the actual programming service will be more refined than the demo tapes. Special demo tapes for sales and promotion use will be produced when the studio complex is complete. . . . [See excerpts from demo tape later in this chapter.]

THE VILLAGE VOICE

Brother John's dulcet tones may catch the fancy of a local advertiser in your market. Although we can't write or produce customized commercials for each station's clients, we will be able to record voice tracks at the going AFTRA rates. The procedure will involve your sending us the copy. We'll send you back the voice track which you can turn into a finished spot using your own production facilities. Because of our tight schedule, we can only allot a few hours a week for customized tracks. . . .

Naturally, Brother John will also record whatever special station material you may need at no charge. Let us know if you need special promos, psa's, or whatever. We'll be glad to help. . . .

POP P,O,P,

As mentioned in last week's newsletter, a "new albums" record store poster is part of our promotional plan. The poster will list 20 new album releases heard on Love, not the top or best-selling LP's—simply 20 new releases in the progressive rock bag which we are playing. . . .

The poster is designed for point-of-purchase display inside the store as well as for the window or door. Thus, we'll be sending each record store 2 copies of the 13" x 44" poster. The actual dimensions may shrink for the sake of printing economy. . . .

Our idea is to print each station's poster here in New York. Since the album list will be the same, this will save typesetting and printing costs.

All we'll have to change is the call letter heading. We will fold the posters down to a 13" x 11" size for flat mailing. . . .

Although the poster will only be issued every 3 to 4 weeks (depending on the amount of good new LP releases), we've been toying with the idea of even handling the entire mailing operation from here, thus saving time and work at the local station. However the poster is handled, we'd like to have it ready to go when programming hits the air (or within a month of that happening). . . .

PONY EXPRESS FROM REDWOOD CITY (NOVEMBER 18)

Our high-speed duplicator arrived last week from Ampex. Installation of the unit should be complete by the end of this week. This was the last major piece of equipment needed to round out our production/duplication facilities. High-speed dubbing will enable us to provide each station with five fresh hours of programming daily. . . .

AIR MAIL FROM NEW YORK CITY

As you read this, station managers will be receiving a stereo dub of the presentation tape mentioned last week. The tape should fully explain the Love programming concept and sales target. It incorporates a telescoped version of actual programming. . . .

STONES/BEATLES PROMOTION READY FOR LANDING

A couple weeks ago we explained that the month-long promotion was on hold for several reasons. Now that promotion is ready to land but in a week-long version instead. Since the actual Love programming will start around January 1st, the idea now is to run Stones/Beatles week between Christmas and New Year's. This way we won't be fighting the pre-Christmas season but taking advantage of the natural lull between holidays. Stones/Beatles week is designated to run during all the hours you regularly plan to air Love. . . .

Both the new Stones and Beatles albums (now available) will be included in the promotion. Following the suggestion of Bob Hennabery, we will probably program the tapes so that one song ("All You Need Is Love") is heard with increasing frequency each day—thus building to a climax and leading into the Love programming kick-off. . . .

SYNDICATION INDICATION

Up till now, we have purposely withheld publicity of any sort about our project. That's why we've been extremely happy to receive several, unsolicited inquiries about syndication of the Love programming. Apparently the grapevine is growing and FM operators in scattered areas have been calling for information. We are definitely planning to syndicate once we can do it on a practical basis for all stations. Syndication will include not only the programming but all the promotional and sales support too. . . .

The key point to remember about syndication is that it will lower our own costs. If Love is successful in the owned markets, it will become a desirable syndication property. Once syndicated to enough markets, the Love programming will cost the owned stations considerably less. . . .

LOVE COMES WITH MATCHING PSA's

Initially, many of the seven hourly commercial spots will be open for public service announcements. We will ship each station customized promos and psa's for national campaigns on a regular basis. As mentioned in our first memo, we will be glad to help you by preparing special promos to your specifications featuring Brother John. . . .

This time out, we're offering to produce customized psa's based on local or regional material which you send us. The idea here is to use the voice of Brother John and production that matches the Love programming for a strictly local public service bit. If you desire such

service (and we recommend it), please send copy and/or recorded
material for excerpting to George Yahraes in New York. . . .

MUSIC, MUSIC, MUSIC

Even though we're not on the air yet, our music list is complete (over
350 cuts) and is being up-dated weekly. New records are reviewed
daily, and promotion men are being seen weekly or whenever they have
something hot. Thus, our music is current, and we're ready to roll. The
tape you receive on Wednesday will be able to contain a record released
on Monday or Tuesday! And since we'll generally go on a record before
the other stations, we may actually be on the air with a new disk weeks
before your "live" competition. . . .

ADD AD THEME

The consumer ad theme under development is: "Have you tried
Love—WXXX Stereo 00.0." The phrase, call letters, and stereo frequency will be the only type in the ads. "Have you tried Love" is also
used frequently on the air. Ad layouts and ideas will be available by
mid-December. No off-air promotion for Stones/Beatles week is
planned. . . .

WEDNESDAY MORNING JITTERS

In the many months we've been developing Love, we have run across
a few items that shook us from a competitive point of view, but none
as much as the article in *Variety*. It's one thing to learn that another
station in one of our markets has gone underground, or that there's
someone named "Brother Love," or some station calling itself "The
Sound of Love," but the headline in *Variety* was the biggest shock of
all.[7] Fortunately after reading it, we're more inclined to smile. Let them
be "radio love" on optical. We'll stick to plain old Love on good old
FM. . . .

VOICING LOVE

Love's sweet medicine.

The excerpts that follow are from the "Love" audio presentation tape
alluded to above. It was narrated by Brother John, with additional vocali-
zation by Allen Shaw.

Love is a feeling. An understanding and caring for humanity. It's the new social awareness expressed in words and music by youth. We will echo the sounds of a nation thinking. You'll hear things you may not like. (Actuality) "What radical students are doing is trying to create change. . . ." Love is people to people radio. . . . [Love's purpose] is to provide a freewheeling approach to foreground excitement for our listeners. The sound is varied, exciting, totally involved with the totally involved. . . . Even the public service announcements have been specially produced to reflect and enforce the overall concept of Love. . . . We're after the young, the college student, the quality-conscious audience, the 18 to 28 year old young adult who can best be *sold* in the Love environment. . . . These are people who are involved in the new way of thinking about life. A life of truth, beauty, and love. . . . These are the people who are into the new music and social thinking, the people who are buying half the record albums, the people who are buying their first insurance policies, the people who are establishing brand preferences, obtaining credit cards, and starting new careers and families. They're living in today's society, but in their own way. . . . Love feels like the way you live today. . . , We are above ground, not underground. . . . We feel society needs to be corrected in a positive way, not destroyed.

ON SELLING THE NEW CULTURE

There will be no such thing as stealing, because everything will be free.
—Jerry Rubin

In 1970, ABC-FM's Spot Sales division prepared its desiderata on the current state of the radio audience marketplace in a promotional piece entitled "A Culture in Evolution." What follows are excerpts from this telling document.

INTRODUCTION

It is difficult to define and completely understand the audience that is listening and responding to progressive and "freeform" programming on stereo FM stations. Yet, the nature of our industry demands that we accept the challenge of audience definition—for this audience must be described in terms of LIFESTYLE, as it parallels demographics. LIFESTYLE is an extra meaningful word to America's youth, for a new generation of young people demand that "life" and "style" be an inseparable quality. . . .

We must clearly define this audience because so many in our industry are continually referring to the "Youth Market" in terms of what it means to them. Everyone seems to have a different idea. We share this

definition of our audience in terms of characteristics, age, specific
"Youth Market" breakdown and purchasing power. At the same time,
we consider our medium, radio, a personal one, reaching intelligent
individuals within an evolving LIFESTYLE. . . .

ITS DIMENSIONS, INFLUENCE, AND OPPORTUNITIES

Today's young people are trendsetters. Never before have they been
so dramatically important in our society. The balance of power is
changing because of sheer numbers. Fifty-nine percent of the population is now under the age of thirty-four. The median age in the United
States is now twenty-eight.

Today's youth are spearheading the development of a LIFESTYLE
uniquely their own, and its impact is being evidenced in every element
of American society. A new culture is emanating. Many choose to call
it a "counterculture," an "alternative culture." But the values, ideals,
concerns and actions of the young people who consider themselves a
part of the LIFESTYLE extend into all segments of the American
culture. The current quality of change points toward recognition of the
roots of a "culture in evolution."

WHAT ARE THE "IDEAL" CHARACTERISTICS
OF THIS NEW CULTURE?

There is a long tradition of studying the extreme to understand the
typical. Thus, we first present this new culture in terms of "ideal"
characteristics.

1. It reverses the cultural priorities of most Americans; it replaces
   competition of the marketplace with cooperation of the small, intimate peer group or commune.
2. It condemns open expression of violence; applauds open expression
   of individuality.
3. It makes human rights more important than property rights; it gives
   higher marks to man than machines.
4. Instead of being goal-oriented toward success, it is expression-ori-
   ented toward fulfillment and gratification.

In defining the culture from these ideals, one creates a market that
practices no discrimination, wages no war, doesn't litter the landscape,
owns worldly goods but doesn't hoard them, commits little crime,
rarely feels hypocrisy or guilt, and almost never comes home drunk.
That is the "ideal," and if it were ever created, it would be a market like
no other market in American economic history.

The idealism of this culture in evolution is possibly best reflected in
the following statement: "We're trying to show people that they can

have their own lifestyle and still live pretty well without having to overturn the government. Everybody's changing, reassessing their values. People are turning on to nurturing things. Pretty soon everybody is going to reject the plastic. And then the United States will be reoriented as a group of thinking individuals rather than a 'homogeneous mass.' "

WHAT ARE THE "REAL" CHARACTERISTICS OF THIS NEW CULTURE?

We have looked at the ideals of the culture in evolution. These ideals have resulted as a direct effect of technology and the currents of change. They represent a response to the recent turn of events. They are influencing, to different degrees, every segment of our culture. We are not viewing a static entity, rather a fluid process.

Young people who consider themselves a part of the new LIFE-STYLE have been most affected by constant change. Why? Because they do not have cultural roots tied to the past in the way that older people do. They have always existed in a state of rapid change. They do not fear its results. They are receptive to new trends and conversions.

They sense a loss, confusion, and estrangement which besets many Americans today. Most alienated Americans are already aware, for example, that the standard of living is rising, that there are more long playing records and quality paperbacks than ten years ago, and many realize that enormous opportunities and challenges confront them. Yet this knowledge is not enough to produce a sense of commitment to American society.

The "new" alienation affects not only those at the bottom of society but those at the top, and it is not only imposed on them by their society, but increasingly "chosen" by them as their dominant response to society. It is an alienation that has few apparent roots in poverty, exclusion, sickness, oppression or lack of choice and opportunity. In many of these youth, alienation is a way of life, an explicit rejection of the values and outlooks of American culture. Though they are rarely able to define alternatives to the conventional way of life of well-adjusted Americans, that life profoundly repels them.

They are spared emotions of the past. They come with a fresh vision. And, they are asking the right questions.

— They want to know why the war to preserve the freedom of South Vietnam kills or injures more than 20,000 civilians of that country each year.

— They want to know why, with the United Nations more than 23 years old, the world is stockpiling nuclear weapons, enough to destroy civilization several times over.

— They want to know why Negroes can fight in America's wars, but can't live in America's suburban neighborhoods.

— They want to know why, in the wealthiest and most highly educated society in history, the poor are expected to break out of the ghetto with no money or education.

They are not only asking disturbing questions, but are suggesting to Americans that the legacy they inherit is worth saving, but not by much. There is no question that the young people of today are a remarkable generation.

We are now discovering the "real" characteristics of the new LIFE-STYLE and its origins. There are a few young people who constitute the "hardcore." They are, if you will, at the far end of the pole—extremely idealistic. They initiate, originate, and to a large extent, give direction. However, the majority of young people in this LIFESTYLE are actually followers. They are attracted to the excitement, the force and energy which surround this new LIFESTYLE. It is positive, it questions, it represents faith, hope, honesty. They want to be in contact with it. They are intrigued, but in many instances, not totally committed. However, future commitment will arise as our society begins to resolve alienations by enjoying diversity and supporting human fulfillment.

WHAT SEGMENTS OF THE "YOUTH MARKET" CONSTITUTE THIS NEW CULTURE?

This new culture or behavioral system directly affects the thoughts and actions of specific segments of the "youth market." The LIFESTYLE age is generally considered to be 18 to 34. The lifestyle represented influences high school students (older teens), college students, young singles and young marrieds.

Teens represent one of the most openminded and receptive marketing segments in the world. In college, personal tastes and brand preferences are formed. It has been established that by 1975, a third of all total consumer dollars will come from households headed by persons with some higher education.

In summary, the combination of young people who constitute the new LIFESTYLE are easily seen as the country's most rapidly expanding group of consumers. Members of this group require and spend more individually than members of younger and older groups.

WHAT PURCHASING POWER DOES THIS LIFESTYLE REPRESENT?

The youth represented within this new LIFESTYLE do spend and would rather live well than die rich. They spend to live in the present rather than save to live in the future. They believe that how one lives today is more important than how one lives tomorrow. They buy what they want when they want it.

And this market is consuming. For example, see-through shirts at $40, leather pants at $80, custom coats at $200. Indeed, the costume that pervades the market from coast to coast is, for the most part, an exclusively designed and exclusively priced look. Their clothes, their stereo equipment, their macrobiotic foods, their personal accessories and furnishings are first rate quality goods.

One reason they can spend at a comparable level to other age groups in our society is that they're not economically committed to one-tenth of the things other age groups are. They're not mortgaged to the hilt. And because this is one kind of influence which they can exert in our society, they release a lot of energy in making purchasing decisions.

The sizeable amount of spendable income from this market is approximately $35 billion annually.

— About $10 billion is available from some seven million college students. Disposable income of college students is considerably estimated at $1,290 per student per year.

— Older teens represent another major bloc of the buying power of this market. Teens have $18 billion of their own and family charge cards.

— The bridal or young marrieds segment of this market is annually over $6.5 billion at retail in 46 merchandise categories.

Major product categories appealing to these people are rapidly emerging. For example, car ownership by young collegians has reached incredible proportions in the last few years.

Consumption of beer and wine is high in this age group. Stereo equipment is a priority purchase. This age group buys a high volume of books and records regularly. They spend considerable amounts on clothing and entertainment. Potential production categories are extensive.

The importance of the young people who make up this LIFESTYLE to manufacturers, retailers, and advertisers is that they are making and can make cash registers ring.

WHAT IS UNIVERSAL AND UNIQUE ABOUT THIS NEW LIFESTYLE?

The young people who constitute the new culture consider music the most creative medium—the universal language. Not too long ago, an interest in music often approached a craze. Now it's an absorption, a total part of the lifestyle. To many, it is the LIFESTYLE—their only contact and identification with the so-called new culture. They feel music is an emotional leap, a concrete rather than a linear experience. Music, they say, is their "common denominator," what draws them together. Music speaks to them, "talks their language." In short, it surrounds them. And directly related to this "surround sound" is the impact of stereo—the way they want to hear their music. For that reason, the bulk of this musical sound is produced and listened to in stereo.

This same group knows about FM radio. FM is the only radio they can listen to in stereo, and it's the only radio serving their needs. FM radio is recreating their music—the cohesive bond of these young people, the motif of their LIFESTYLE.

WHERE ARE YOUTH, LIFESTYLE, MONEY, AND MUSIC COMBINED?

The growth of progressive rock FM stations has been impressive. Comparison of the 1968 and 1970 FM Programming Surveys of the National Association of FM Broadcasters indicates a tremendous growth of the progressive rock format within a comparatively brief period of time.

Within the top ten markets there are currently 21 progressive rock FM stations; within the top 20 markets there are 32 FM progressives. Many of these stations are beginning to recognize the importance of this audience as potential consumers. Progressive rock promises major growth in audience as well as advertising dollars. And the trend is just beginning.

ABC-FM Spot Sales represents FM stations that reach young people who make up this new LIFESTYLE. They reach young people psychologically inclined to think and feel—and buy—in the same way. It's a market which includes college students and recent graduates who know and appreciate social and media change, an audience socially aware, active, concerned and honest.

The objective of ABC Spot Sales has been to represent stations that are developing a type of radio that is totally involving and meaningful to the new culture. By getting into lifestyle, a type of radio has been established that serves the needs, feels the moods and communicates effectively with those who are a part of the LIFESTYLE. They are into progressive rock. The music and words are meaningful to them. Progressive rock mirrors their moods, their dreams and frustrations, and motivates their actions.

The programming of ABC-FM stations is directed to youthful involvement and participation in a "total experience," an experience created from elements of the unpredictable, i.e., classical, folk, rock, blues, jazz, talk and discussion.

WHAT ADVERTISING APPROACH REACHES THIS AUDIENCE?

As for advertising, never has a generation been so critical and so mature in its criticism of advertising. The traditionally accepted objectives and creative forms of advertising will come under increasingly severe and sophisticated attack. This is a sceptical group and they are not easily impressed.

Many young people in this LIFESTYLE say they're not influenced by advertising. That may be true, but nearly all of them are alive and attuned to its possibilities. They've been stung by bad advertising that tries to co-opt their values into worthless products they neither want nor need, and they've been abused by advertising that's basically a rip-off. An advertising rip-off is a campaign that tries to worm its way into the culture and doesn't make it.

They demand honesty! Yet, caution must be used in describing an "honest" campaign. Too many advertisers today are hung up on creating honest campaigns that are dull, uninspired, lacklustre, and boring. They don't stimulate. This audience loves to be amused and gratified. A campaign shouldn't lose sight of its primary selling function, but it should be fun.

Anyone who would use our medium for youth-directed commercials must accept the responsibility it entails. The advertiser approaching this market must be above suspicion. The protests arising from unwitting blunders will be as prompt as if they were stirred up by a conscious exploitation and will probably hurt more.

Advertising should not be the scapegoat for all those things found distasteful in our society any more than advertising should be given credit for those aspects of American life holding promise for the future. But one thing is certain—advertising and the powers that be must direct themselves to the challenge of the "culture in evolution."

NOTES

1. Theodore Roszak, *The Making of the Counter Culture* (New York: Doubleday, 1969), p. 17.

2. David Caute, *The Year of the Barricades: A Journey Through 1968* (New York: Harper and Row, 1988), p. xiii.

3. E. B. Weiss,"Youth Junks the 'Junk Culture,' " *Advertising Age*, September 7, 1970, p. 35.

4. Peter Fornatale and Joshua Mills, *Radio in the Television Age* (New York: Overlook Press, 1980), p. 134.

5. *SAM*, June 5, 1970, p. 29.

6. Mike Gormley, "WABX Is David, Knocking 'Em Dead with Rock," *Detroit Free Press*, August 9, 1970, p. 7.

7. The headline referred to appeared in the November 13, 1968, issue of *Variety*. It read: "U.K.'s Radio Love as Optical Station," and it told of a proposed laser-optical system for transmitting broadcast signals.

Chapter Five

Something's Happening Here

Political society exists for the sake of noble action.

—Aristotle

Those kids, why do they hate me so much?

—Richard Nixon

The whole world's watching.

—Chicago protesters

Commercial underground radio drew breath from the social and cultural dynamics of the period. When the tumult of the late 1960s and early 1970s gave way to the relative tranquility of the middle and late seventies, the format lost much of its relevance and vitality and quickly faded from the scene. What had given underground radio its primary impetus and inspiration, besides occurrences within the broadcasting industry, was the steady, if not unrelenting, political actions and counteractions which held much of the nation in thrall. Massive antiwar demonstrations, widespread race rioting, and bloody clashes with police helped sustain commercial underground radio's altruistic view of itself—a view shared by many of its fans, if not its critics.

Not everyone perceived the commercial radio medium as capable of possessing such ideological qualities and motives. Whereas underground broadcasters often felt themselves to be an integral part of the so-called movement of the time, they were frequently looked upon as simply part and parcel of the saccharine whole. In other words, radio was just, well, radio. Observed noted economist John Kenneth Galbraith, "There is an insistent ndency among solemn social scientists to think [of] any institution which features rhymed and singing commercials . . . voices urging highly improbable enjoyments, as inherently trivial."[1]

> *Carla Brooks Johnston:* You know, a lot was happening in the 60s that commercial underground stations subordinated to their sex, drugs, and rock and roll message. There were other issues too—the poor, the blacks, women, the gentle folk who joined Rachel Carson's environmental movement and "the small is beautiful" drive. The entire society was upset, except for the older generation who survived the Depression, won the war, and couldn't understand why the kids weren't grateful and obedient. For many of these other "movements," there was music and radio, too. Perhaps folk music more than rock—political folk music, which was more likely to be heard on the public, noncommercial stations—was the real underground radio medium for many of us.

Even Abbie Hoffman doubted to what extent the commercial media could contribute to the counterculture's cause given its inherently entrepreneurial underpinnings and the political powers that be. In his autobiographical *Soon to Be a Major Motion Picture*, and in numerous other publications, Hoffman balks at the notion that radio, television, and the press are free to disseminate the truth about what is really happening in the world. If you think this, he warns, "you haven't thought about it enough."[2]

> *Tim Powell:* I have been choked for years on the digestive gases of those people who would try to make the birth of this kind of radio a hallowed occasion or anything more than it is. I find particularly offensive the attempts to imagine the evolutionary development of a non-single oriented rock format into the "beating of the tribal drum," a potent and particularly sickminded romantic glorification of what was as inevitable as the evolution of Top 40 in the 1950s.

> *Stefan Ponek:* After working in underground for a number of years, I actually moved back to pop radio, which in some perverse way seemed more honest to me by that time.

> *Lee Abrams:* These stations mostly pretended to serve the people. They were self-serving, elitist, and ultimately destructive because the people who ran them only wanted to serve a small minority.

Larry Miller: That's not accurate. Saying that denies the reality. Look, I don't think for a minute that these stations forced the United States to get out of Vietnam, for example, or singlehandedly brought peace back to the streets. Nixon staged the end of the war, along with lowering both the voting and drinking ages, just in time to assure his reelection. The war ended when he and Kissinger decided to end it, not a minute before—underground radio or no underground radio.

New voices spoke to the young in a language that baffled those too old to listen.

—*Life* magazine, December 1969

In his memoir, deejay Jim Ladd posits the view that underground radio contributed significantly to what he refers to as the counterculture's "vision of the promised land."[3] And Scoop Nisker observes in his autobiography that

for a few years before the profiteers took over, KSAN and stations like it across the nation were rightfully called "underground radio." We promoted antigovernment protests, we preached against capitalism and the Judeo-Christian religions, we openly encouraged the use of marijuana and LSD, and, of course, we played the music to accompany all these activities. We were tribal radio, filling the heads of American youth with a call to sex, drugs, rock 'n' roll and revolution.[4]

Allen Shaw: Politically, commercial underground radio was saying "fuck you" to the establishment, and that struck a chord in the hearts of its listeners. This was "their" radio station.

Roland Jacopetti: Undeniably, underground radio, certainly KSAN, was enormously influential at the time. When you met people and told them you worked at KSAN, they were almost always impressed. Certainly the station shared the phenomenon that the Grateful Dead exemplified. That freaks just like you—bushy haired, joint smoking, acid dropping, jobless, untrained, disrespectful, radical, and hippie— could actually join the ranks of the elite. It was possible to tune a radio station that was run by hippies, announced by hippies, supported by hippie advertisers, with music sung by hippies. People just like you, or pretty much.

Allen Shaw: In our most idealized fantasies, we knew that we were an on-air expression of a major political and cultural revolution. We were the baby boomers making our big break from all prior generations, especially the "silent" generation of our parents. We were flexing our muscles in huge numbers with a new look, a new sound, and a new value system. Our FM stations were a daily electronic conduit through which the music, news of the antiwar movement, and [the] credo of the new value system of the Woodstock Generation was being fed, as if fuel, to millions of fellow soldiers in each of our markets. We knew at ABC-FM that we were, as unlikely as it was, the largest corporate entity broadcasting the drumbeat of the Flower Children Tribe over powerful FM radio stations in New York, Pittsburgh, Detroit, Chicago, Houston, Los Angeles, and San Francisco. There was a certain amount of headiness in our attitude. It wasn't easy radio. On a day-to-day basis, there were problems and fears to deal with. In 1970 the Vietnam War was reaching its peak of unpopularity. The Nixon administration was beginning to put direct pressure on the media to treat it and the war more "fairly." President Nixon was already looking to the 1972 elections and had his "plumbers" at work. Vice President Agnew was attacking the media almost daily. Nixon also had Herb Klein, whose job was, among other things, to regularly meet with the network media brass to assess the job they were doing with respect to reporting on the Nixon administration. Nixon must have known that the only leverage against the networks was the FCC. It was an implied threat (never actually acted upon to my knowledge) that if a broadcasting company didn't please the president, it would have problems with the commission. It was also known that the FBI was keeping files on all the antiwar activists in the country, plus anyone else whose views might be interpreted as "dangerous," as Daniel Schorr and Daniel Ellsberg found out. It was a charged atmosphere to do the kind of radio we were doing, but it also energized us.

Whatever is morally necessary must be made politically possible.
—Eugene McCarthy, 1968

Dan Carlisle: Sitting in the studio at WABX at night, thirty-three floors above the street, I would look out into the vast spread of light and wonder if I was helping shape future leaders or just playing records. Over the years, I have received some answers to that haunting question. While working at KLOS in Los Angeles I received calls from former Detroiters who wanted to chat about their experience listening to WABX and also to let me know it was a powerful force of "good" in their lives. Two of these folks were surgeons practicing medicine in L.A. Sometimes just regular folks living their lives called me and gave me the distinct impression that I helped to broaden their horizons concerning music and social thought. I know of at least one federal judge who counts listening to WABX among his formative life events. Perhaps the following story will best sum up the positive influence. Gerry Lubin worked at WABX during its earliest period, 1967 to 1971, and told me that not many years ago a woman approached him at a social gathering and talked enthusiastically about the station. She then said, "Actually, were it not for WABX I might have ended up a cheerleader."

Russ Gibb: We raised the consciousness level of the kids in both practical and profound ways. We tuned them in to the Vietnam War debacle and the environment. We really put them in touch with things that AM never did, but we also did them a disservice. We talked about all the things that brought us together. We knew a lot of things sucked, but in retrospect, I don't think we were in touch with the things that made us great—the things that made us unique.

Dwight Douglas: When you're young, you sometimes miss things or don't catch their full import. When I started in radio, I had the great opportunity to work at a high-powered FM station in Pittsburgh—WAMO. We only played progressive rock from 9 P.M. to 4 A.M. and 1 P.M. to 4 P.M. At 4 A.M. the station aired gospel music until 6 A.M., then it played blues and jazz the balance of the time. The rock portion of the programming was called "Radio Free Pittsburgh." I did the midnight to 4 A.M. show and called myself Gemini. One night a group of anti-war protesters were arrested after a demonstration at a local draft board member's house. When they were being arraigned in court, the police turned off the lights and beat them up. They later became known as the "Pittsburgh 12." I happened to be on the air that night. After cueing up a record, I looked up and there were twenty people standing in my studio. It was 2 A.M. They wanted to go on the air and tell the story. I talked them into coming back the next day to

A psychedelic station poster for a psychedelic time.

go on a special talk show. I then read the wire copy of the story and promoted the show. I explained to the protesters that there would be a larger audience during the day, and this satisfied them. "Radio Free Pittsburgh" was short-lived. After three months of some excellent radio, the Black Panthers told the owner that if he didn't change the station back to all R&B, they would blow it up. We were all fired, and my first experience with new FM ended. I was making $62 a week and happy.

Dusty Street: There was a community out there that really needed to have its concerns addressed, and Tom Donahue came along and created a station that did that. Talk about real public service radio, we were it, and it made a difference in the lives of many people. I feel privileged to have been a part of it.

Bobby Seale: Commercial underground stations, like KMPX and KSAN, lent their airwaves to the Black Panther Party in various positive ways. They served as an extension to the underground print media, including our own publication. These radio stations performed a service to the Party, which aided it in its humane mission. They were willing to give us their microphones for a cause that everyone else in the mainstream thought was evil and tyrannical. Underground radio stations were a part of the revolution that sought to enlighten the world and inform it of the cruel and horrible injustices perpetrated against the people.

John Gehron: These stations became the voice of the most vocal (albeit smallest) part of the baby boomer population, and they impacted music, clothing, advertising, and politics.

Bonnie Simmons: We were radio without contempt for our audience, which was an uncommon phenomenon at the time. Part of the beauty, too, was that we didn't have a real sense of our importance. To us, we were just playing music and talking with our friends.

If any demonstrator ever lays down in front of my car, it'll be the last car he'll ever lay down in front of.

—George C. Wallace, 1968

Ed Shane: We were having fun, but there was this sense of social awareness—the war in Vietnam, the garbage workers' strike in Atlanta, the gay movement in San Francisco. Through the music and through the ability to add "editorial" commentary on the air, the issues our audience cared about were covered. And, too, there was a great sense of community. We were part of something that lots of people shared. I stepped on stage as emcee of the Atlanta Pop Festival, about to introduce a new band, Chicago Transit Authority. They had been booked as part of the festival's deal to get Blood Sweat and Tears, and the guys in Chicago weren't too happy about being there. "Nobody knows us," they complained before they went on. "Don't worry," I said. "You'll be surprised." My introduction referenced the titles of songs that had been played on WPLO-FM. The crowd roared its approval, and Chicago responded with a tight set. The record industry sure took notice of those of us who were early in the underground format. Where else could they get such willing exposure for their new product? Most of the record promotion representatives who called on me in Atlanta wanted opinions on the new releases. They admitted they didn't know the music very well. No one really did. Most of us were making it up as we went along, learning anew from every release, every concert. I'm sure I'm not alone in having been treated like an expert by the guys in the record industry who were supposed to be the experts. No one tried to create the "mystique" I mentioned earlier. It just happened because of all the forces in alignment. Yet the mystique was a factor of working within the station environment. At WPLO-FM, we knew we didn't make the magic, but we sure felt it as the result of our work. The societal effect was in the politicization of many of the stations and some of the music. Commercial underground radio offered information on issues that would not otherwise have been treated on commercial radio. It created awareness and even prompted some people into action. It gave the U.S. a healthy sounding board for issues both local and national. It underscored the diversity that America was founded upon. Here I should say something specific about the "radio culture." The commercial underground format innovated many programming techniques that are in use today. The idea behind "match flow," for example. We did thematic and compatible key segues to show our skills in matching music. Who would have known that the idea also enhanced time spent listening? The idea of playing several songs in a row with no talk was anathema to Top 40 radio, but it was a staple of the underground format. There was the sense of accomplishing something mighty creative. Not just disc jockey work, but weaving songs together in progression to make a statement or a theme. This original radio genre contributed many things to both the industry and the culture. Foremost, for those of us working in this unique form of radio, it liberated us to explore and experiment, and the public appreciated the results. Others appreciated what we were trying to do. John Lennon came on the air with me while I was at WGLD in Chicago. He shared things with us, like bootleg tapes of the Beatles, because he felt we were on the same wavelength.

The freedom and independence of expression so cherished by underground staffers were the very things that propelled the counterculture movement itself. Deejays at these stations imagined themselves trekking through the airwaves of America on a sacred quest for meaning and grace not unlike that sought by Peter Fonda in a defining motion picture of the time, *Easy Rider*. Like Fonda's character, underground deejays were just "trying to get [their] thing together" in a world rife with uncertainty, while underground stations battled with questions concerning their very nature. Observed Scoop Nisker, "KSAN couldn't escape that basic contradiction: we were attacking the establishment while being supported by it, and worse, our rebel broadcasting was beginning to make big profits for a giant corporation."[5]

Dusty Street: We were doing valid work, but we did realize that some essential contradictions were at work. That doesn't diminish the contributions made by these stations. In fact, it distinguishes them all the more.

Scoop Nisker: To its credit, and despite the negative internal forces at work, KSAN served as a communications center for many counterculture groups, like the Weather Underground, Youth Brigade, and the Symbionese Libera-

The gang on the waterbed in the KSAN lobby pose for a promotional photo. The nude was a paid model.

tion Army. It took courage and conviction to do this, but that's what the station was about until the mid-1970s.

Larry Miller: Mostly we reflected the radical leftist liberal political point of view. Among other things, our agenda included the legalization of dope, racial equality, and the termination of the Vietnam conflict.

I daresay the native value of a good thing is only weakened by claims on its behalf.

—Daniel Berrigan, S.J.

Kate Ingram: These stations rolled the counterculture into the mainstream and gave the baby boomer generation its first taste of legitimacy.

Roland Jacopetti: When I contemplate the question concerning what these stations contributed most to the American scene, I think music. Certainly it was underground radio that helped put less sanitized rock out there. It was really the progenitor of the outrageous metal arena acts, of Jim Morrison taking out his dick on stage, of all that was politically incorrect (for the time)—outrageous, risky, and over the edge. Pop radio in the 1960s was way less far out, and somehow there's not a clear path from a hyper AM jock playing the cotton-candy hits and MC5 taking a shit on the stage. We have a direct analogy in the 1990s with innumerable strangely named bands playing tiny gigs here and there, being interviewed by the zines, but receiving no air play beyond the university stations. I feel that underground radio, particularly in San Francisco, gave rock and roll legitimacy, and that if it weren't for KSAN and its loyal following, Bill Graham and Chet Helmes would never have been as successful as they were with the Fillmore and the Avalon. Underground delivered rock music to an audience that wouldn't necessarily turn out for the Dead in Golden Gate Park or a big dance at the Fillmore but would certainly turn their radio on, smoke a doobie, lie back and say, "Oh, wow!"

Allen Shaw: The Fillmore for me is such a touchstone of that era. A night at the Fillmore East was a combination of danger, communal warmth, and great music. Located in a rough section of New York City's East Village, menacing-looking bikers lined the streets as you made your way to the auditorium. Once inside, one was engulfed in a sweet haze of weed and incense. An atmosphere of Woodstock in miniature prevailed. Most patrons of Fillmore were authentic Greenwich Village hippies complete with long hair, long beards, psychedelically colored headbands, elaborate beads around their necks, and earrings. Some couples would bring their babies with them to see bands like Jethro Tull or the Incredible String Band. The relatively small auditorium created a tight, warm connection between hippies and their minstrels.

Raechel Donahue: Music was a driving and defining force in the sixties. It actually had a part in altering the path of history. It was a phenomenal time, and we were doing phenomenal radio.

John Gorman: From LBJ to Nixon on, there was no shortage of material. The unreal and wild events of that period inspired the most amazing rock music ever, and we were there to provide it a much needed venue.

In a 1996 article in the *New York Times*, Jon Pareles reflected back on the extraordinary relationship that baby boomers had with their rock music in the late 1960s and early 1970s:

> We had of course invented youth, rebellion, idealism, sex, recreational drug use and the music that went with all of it. Like pop consumers before us, we found songs that summed up our longings and our resentments. But we were sure that those songs weren't just entertainment: they were the foundation of a new culture, a counterculture. And we decided that the musicians we listened to were exalted creatures. They were no longer mere performers but artists, perhaps even shamans, leading a revolution in consciousness.[6]

Lee Abrams: For me, I suppose, the most convincing or concrete evidence of the impact of underground radio is the present-day success of FM. It really opened the door to enormous opportunities and possibilities for the medium.

Thom O'Hair: The FM band had been around for quite a while before these stations came along and jump-charged it. Stereo had been around for nearly a decade too, but people were not exactly lining up to buy FM stereo receivers. The market penetration for this product was extremely low. When these stations came along with their progressive sound, it motivated people to go out and purchase an FM set. They weren't cheap either, often hundreds of dollars for a good one. The listener made a commitment just to access what was on FM. Around the time of this format, many new FM stereo outlets were debuting around the country, and things began percolating for the medium.

Al Wilson: I'd concur that the major contribution that commercial underground radio made to the culture was that it established the commercial FM band as the more prominent of the two radio bands. It took a while, but it happened. Commercial underground radio also established stereo broadcasting (as opposed to mono) as the standard for FM music stations.

Ed Shane: It was seminal to FM radio in the United States. The FM band had lain fallow for so many years. Something had to bring audience to FM. While there might have been other ideas on the horizon, this was the one that worked. It created attention and interest among an all-new set of radio users, who really loved what they were hearing.

LOVE LETTER

Worked up into a total frenzy, bordering on electric Buddha nirvana total acid freak cosmic integration—one with the universe.

—Frank Zappa, 1968

The following fan letter was sent to Brother John in November 1969.

Dear John,

I'm beginning to feel a new kind of feeling—beginning to sing a new kind of song. I just want to tell you about Thanksgiving night in this household for a few minutes if you've got a few minutes. It really was the ultimate! There were seven of us who got together in our rec room to dig the scene. My dude and I, my sister, Pam and her dude, my brother, Mick and his chick, and my little brother, Dave. About 7 P.M. we made our stuffed excuses and made for the rec room. Eric, my love, brought his super cool stereo radio, and we set it up against the far wall, out of sight, and hid the speakers as best we could. Mick built a huge, roaring fire, burning apple and beech logs. The apple logs made a great smell and the beech burned blue. It was a beautiful fire. Then we tuned in LOVE and turned the lights out. We sat hand and hand or laid in front of the fireplace, a little restless and excited. Some of us tried a little loving in our impatience. Somewhere around Hendrix, I tuned in. The others came to in time to catch Guthrie and a few fabulous laughs at Alice's Restaurant. After that, it was all you.

It broke quick, and it broke heavy. Joplin had us clapping and roaring. Donovan had us singing along with him. There were a few tambourines laying around, and the clinking sound and ensuing rhythms picked up and died out as the mood struck the music makers. The Iron Butterfly caused us all to become drummers, and the beat rang from the floor, walls, chairs, and whatever else was handy. It seemed as though whenever things reached a pitch where there just wasn't anything better, the clapping would shower over us and poof . . . a miracle.

Mick, being just 10 years old, was called to bed somewhere near 10 o'clock. It could have been a catastrophe, but not this time, man. Just as he was getting ready to make a teary-eyed exit, the Stones cut loose. And who could have a better send off than the super cool sound of "Satisfaction"? We settled down to get it all. We felt drunk on sound. The Doors, Traffic, The Cream, and Blind Faith—we were gone! The fire just kept flickering against the walls, all psychedelic like. And somebody's foot was shadow projected on the wall about two feet high, beating out a constant rhythm. In the dark, Eric was glassy-eyed, and I was so wound up I wasn't sure I wouldn't be sick.

The fire died down glowing blue and smelling like some kind of incense. And then the Creedence! One pair of eyes flew open and the tape recorder went on. All tambourines were put onto instant action. Creedence came out of the walls and from under the couch. "Proud Mary" grabbed at everyone's gut and took them for a joyride.

From the roar of cheers and squeals, six heavy bodies staggered from under the ruins, thinking they had glimpsed the full extent of Heaven. Then the Beatles shattered the air, and we were flying again, about as high and as gone as six people can get in one night. "I get high with a little help from my friends" and with that we let out a cheer. Then we clasped hands in a circle as "Hey Jude" lifted from earth. Mick whispered that when he closed his eyes the music took him and he didn't even know who or what or where he was. None of us did. We felt only the touch and closeness of each other and the Jude sound vibrating in our minds. Then it was over. No one moved. The fire gave out one last burst of protest and died. "Geeze," said Pam. "If God didn't create rock, he sure missed his claim to glory, didn't he?" And then Eric said, "Wow! Wow! I ain't never been that high on anything. I just ain't never had a high like that!" Suddenly I remembered that I had to be at work at 6 A.M. the next day, so I got up to go to bed feeling a little dizzy and vaguely spent and climaxed. Like nothing in this world could ever be as great as the highest high on LOVE!

> Thanks, man—well you know . . .
>
> Kimmy

COMMUNAL AIR

Oh, what fun . . . at the radio bizarre.

Radio stations are not typically characterized by their sanity. They are, to say the least, unusual establishments. They employ a diverse mix of people who often have little in common with one another. The administrative and sales areas commonly think that deejays and programmers reside on the weird side of the moon, and vice versa. Of all the many kinds of radio stations, perhaps none inspired such a profound sense of two distinct communities as did underground operations. When the air staff at KMPX felt their program director, Tom Donahue, was being mistreated by management, they went on strike in his behalf. Ultimately, they relocated en masse with Donahue to another Bay Area radio station, KSAN. The tribe stayed together, leaving the evil empire of money-hungry bosses and owners behind, or so they thought.

> *Raechel Donahue:* We were a tight bunch. Family might say. We didn't have much at the start, but we did have one another and a strong sense of unity and purpose.

> *Dave Dixon:* You really had to stick together or get screwed. Some of these managers were doozers. For example, John Detts became the boss at WABX because he had the keys.

> *Kate Ingram:* We were extremely supportive of one another on the programming side, and there was such a high level of enthusiasm for what we were about.

> *Roland Jacopetti:* Having fun was really the main idea, and that's a big reason why the station sounded so good. There was tremendous synergy. Working at KSAN was the most fun I ever had that I got paid for. Like at any station, there were always disgruntled sponsors who were never happy with what we did for them. Of course, they could never explain what it was they actually wanted. We had

to deal with clients who were convinced that they were embryo radio personalities and wanted to voice their own spots, but despite that we had as much fun as anybody making a living.

Tim Powell: It wasn't much of a living dollar-wise, so you had to be deriving something else from the experience. One month, the program director and I figured out what the nut was for KMPX—salaries, rent, and utilities included. It was $3,600 a month. God, that was a pretty sick statistic, but things kept running. We got paid in freedom, and that was an extraordinary bonus. Certainly the spartan accommodations weren't a perk. KMPX had the darkest studios I've ever seen, but we made the most of it. It was actually wonderful. There was an engineers' area, which was the studio used by the combo jocks, with an announce booth across double-glassed windows. The audio console was placed facing the announcer. Buddha (an announcer, not a God) set up a color organ in the announce booth. He then covered the walls with fluorescent Day-Glo paint, with freeform paintings. There was a Thermin in this room, although I never figured out what it actually did. You'd sit in the room, on the air, and there would be the frequencies of your voice splashed in red, blue, green, and yellow on the fluorescent spray paint. It was mesmerizing, so you really had to concentrate on the copy, or the microphone, or the vu meters.

Roland Jacopetti: It could get pretty crazy. Freedom can be a breeding ground for the bizarre as well as the sublime. One of my favorite KSAN stories had to do with a nude photograph of the staff. One of the early waterbed entrepreneurs had given the station a king-size bed that we put in the station's lobby. He brought a shapely woman in to photograph her on the waterbed for some kind of print ad he was doing. Now here's an indication of how wacked out it was. Suddenly a large portion of the KSAN staff joined her on the bed for a group photo. I can't really remember if this had been planned or what, but there must have been some kind of notice to get all these people together in one place during the day. Anyway, after the photo was shot, it seemed a logical next step for us to get naked for another round of photos. Willis Duff, the station manager, departed the group at the first mention of this impropriety. Once we shed our garments, several photos were taken.

Willis eventually came back into the lobby only to encounter a bunch of his paid staff cavorting naked. This set him off. "Come on, you guys!" he yelled. "Get your clothes on and get out of here. I've got people coming in a few minutes!" Without a second's pause, every bare-assed person on the waterbed cried out in perfect unison, "We *are* the people!" Willis threw his hands up in defeat and strode out of the room.

Dave Pierce: It was a weird kind of brotherhood that flourished in underground stations. Stories abound. For example, there was the one about Charles Laquidara, who went on to dominate the airwaves in Boston for decades. Of course, this was when he was a kid really. As the tale goes, when he had his fill of life at KPPC-FM way back in the 1960s, he put the Beatles' "White Album" on a turntable, climbed into his ancient Dodge, and headed for the airport. Once there, he abandoned his car, with the keys still in the ignition, and headed East, leaving us wondering what the hell had happened to him. Eventually we knew. After all this time, he's still one of my best friends.

Allen Shaw: Working in commercial underground radio was, above all, exciting. There certainly was a sense of our being on the edge. Given the kinds of statements we were making on our FM stations on a daily basis, I eventually became somewhat paranoid. All of our FM stations ran a Fourth of July special in 1970 entitled "Self Evident Truths." This was a program we produced ourselves and felt strongly about. It juxtaposed statements from Nixon, Agnew, and LBJ against quotes about freedom and the Constitution from early American presidents and patriots, as well as some of the most politically searing rock songs of the day. It was a hard-hitting hour of anti-Nixon and anti–Vietnam war theater. Bill Greeley of *Variety* magazine apparently heard the program we did and ran a major article in the July 8 edition. The piece, called "Radio Nation vs. TV Nation," contrasted the Bob Hope–hosted Independence Day TV network program with our radio program. While we were flattered by Greeley's critical praise of our offering compared with the TV program, I was overcome by a wave of paranoia. What would Herb Klein think of it? What would the corporate brass think of it? Would the FBI investigate who was behind the creation of the program? Would my phones be bugged, my office burglarized? Would my boss have a little chat with the company's chairman about his left-wing activist FM division? My personal paranoia reached a peak a week or so later. Alex Bennett was doing a no-holds-barred, politically expressive morning show on our New York station, WPLJ. One particular morning he had Abbie Hoffman as his guest. I had gone down to the studio to meet Hoffman. As I left the studio to return to my office on another floor, the elevator door opened. There stood Herb Klein. He didn't seem to recognize me, so I got on and rode up to my floor and made a quick exit from the elevator. Herb went up to what I assumed was the chairman's office to have his talk about our FM stations. I waited in my office all day for the phone call from above, but it never came. I had apparently dodged a Nixon bullet. I did get a call from ABC lobby security a few weeks later asking me if I knew who had illegally parked a VW bus right in front of the building on Avenue of the Americas. "What makes you think I would know about this?" I asked. The guard suggested I come down and take a look for myself. When I arrived at the lobby level, I saw an old, beat-up VW bus covered in psychedelic paint, replete with peace symbols and marijuana leaves. I realized how widespread the reputation and image of my FM division had become among all employees at the network. The van obviously belonged to one of our WPLJ disc jockeys who, being late for his shift, parked defiantly and illegally directly in front of the building. What the hell, he was one of mine. The one thing that united us all was the music. Although I was not aware of it at the time, we were living in the middle of the making of rock history. I recall when the record promoters would deliver their new album releases, there'd be a real hum amongst the group. We were witnessing together the beginnings of some legendary rock bands. It was like sharing in a birth. I remember having the first Led Zeppelin album tossed on my desk along with an inflatable silver-colored zeppelin, which I took home to my three-year-old son. I remember listening to the album and being struck by the extraordinary sound of Jimmy Page's guitar work and Robert Plant's voice. While I felt this was something special, I had no idea how big this band was going to become. Then there was the night I was working late in my office at 1330 Avenue of the Americas and Al Kooper dropped by with a tape he had just brought from a recording session at Columbia Records studio down the street. He thought I might want to play a song from a new album he and James Guercio had just produced in which he used a lot of brass arrangements within a rock base. I put the tape on the machine and heard "Beginnings" for the first time. This would not be Chicago's last album. It really was an exceptional time.

Tim Powell: Well, they weren't all halcyon moments. Underground had its share of loonies. Guess this harkens back to the freedom thing. There is a price, as they say. Some of it makes you laugh and some of it makes you scratch your head. Later in my stay at KMPX, I came in one day to do my midnight air shift. There is an absence of spirit that occurs when a radio station is off the air, especially in the main studio. I walked in and the station was definitely off the air. The guy who I was relieving was furiously going through the file of singles. I asked him what was happening as I noticed the raw carrier was still being generated. In 1968, all the singles that a station like KMPX needed were kept in a box that held about 200 if filled, and this fellow, who later would become a national promotion director for a major record label, was furiously digging through it. He couldn't find a record he'd promised to air next. It was "Jesus Is Coming" by the Sons of Champlin. Eventually, I reached over the guy and opened the microphone and said, "We'll be right back with more of Marcel Marceau's new album after we remind you that you're listening to KMPX-FM 106.9, San Francisco." This freaked the guy out, because he was high on coot. Finally he figured out that the record was gone and shortly after that, he was too. For a while there was a crew of yahoos imported from Hawaii at KMPX. I wouldn't give their memory the effort it would take to recall their names, fools that they were, except for the lengendary Gus Gossett, who ended up with a bullet in his head in the backseat of a car somewhere in the Deep South. He started oldies on CBS-FM and stole the record library from KMPX right before heading to New York. Tom Swift, Rick Beban, and myself stole them back from his apartment while he was on the air. These fools loved the "underground" thing and used to say "KMPX under San Francisco" like they were broadcasting from a sewer or something. I even have a poster from that era in my attic featuring this cathedral-style radio with a very nasty, frowning face and a hand coming out of the speaker grill. In the hand is a small human form, and the radio is resting on a bunch of writhing bodies, not unlike you would imagine Hell to be. These were some bad folks. They had absolutely no knowledge of the music. They were not from the mainland and had no idea what was going on. Everyone told me that these guys got to the States and went drug nuts. Taking a ton of acid. Downs and coke and stuff. One reportedly left the station when a miniature dragon materialized on his desk and told him to leave. Gus did hard time in federal penitentiaries before getting offed. They thought Chad and Jeremy were cool. Probably too much acid in Hawaii. They were from the wrong side of the island and just didn't have a clue. The KMPX strike never really left that station. Anton LeVay did something. He's the big satanic witch in San Francisco. He wouldn't put a curse on people, but he cursed something. Anton Szvandor LeVay. Now there's an odd character from the underground vault. A real nutcase. Weirdness wasn't only confined to the station. As a staff, we had seen a lot of bad stuff at free concerts, too. Not everything had that "Woodstock" spirit. We tried to discourage listeners from attending Altamont, knowing that security would be shaky and the atmosphere charged. We gave directions, as we didn't want people to change stations, but we warned them to stay away. A family feud was brewing. Well, three folks died and a few months later several of us at the station were canned because, now get this, we didn't have the "Woodstock" vibe. This wasn't the first time I got fired. When I started at KMPX, there was a guy who was on before me who would close his show by telling listeners that he was going to Golden Gate Park to get high and he'd love them to join him. There was a lot that could be said on the air. Yes, freedom! However, I got fired once for putting a telephone up to an open mike on the overnight show because someone allegedly said "fuck." The cops in Berkeley had just killed a kid over a plot of land known as "People's Park." I was fired another time because, while interviewing the Fraternity of Man, who did "Don't Bogart That Joint," I read a psa about venereal disease and a band member said "Or fuck a sheep." Management said I caused this to happen. Yes, freedom! But always rehired. There was a lot of palaver about the Vietnam War, but it wasn't a big deal. In truth, we ignored most of the current events and just grooved along.

Roland Jacopetti: Getting fired was a common underground radio experience. But the family usually got you
back in there or somewhere else. In 1971 Willis Duff sacked
me. Paul Boucher had made a mess of the PD's job, and
Will wanted to put him back in production. My technical
skills were never my long suit, particularly in the early days,
so Willis was adamant about my leaving. I knew some
people who had gone over to KSFX, ABC's attempt to
compete with KSAN, so I called the PD and was invited to
join the station. Radio is a sort of extended family anyway,
but underground was especially so.

LIVING ON ETHER

At the Bohemian fringe of our disaffected youth culture, all roads lead
to psychedelia.

—Theodore Roszak

Nobody ever leaves the bus.

—Ken Kesey

There were many anthems near and dear to the heart of underground
on-air personnel, but Timothy Leary's ("Dr. Trips"—"the most dangerous
man alive," according to Richard Nixon) dramatic and outrageous summons
to the "hip" world to "Turn On, Tune In, Drop Out" was for most a true
rallying call. According to the high priest of LSD, the phrase was to serve
as a mantra to action (or inaction), which was to be practiced and repeated
continually if one was to grow into a fully evolved state of being. Repeating
this process did not pose a particular problem for many undergrounders,
who used drugs routinely as an integral part of their lifestyle, both on and
off the air.

In 1970 the *New York Times* reported that a random survey of underground
radio stations found that drug use was central to the listening experience of
its audience. The article noted that television personality Art Linkletter, whose
daughter had died from a drug overdose, was determined to reform these rogue
broadcast operations. Two years before the launch of Linkletter's antidrug
crusade, Lewis Yablonsky declared in *The Hippie Trip* that "drug taking is an
integral part of the New Community and its philosophy."[7]

Charles Laquidara: Drugs were a fact of life, outside these
stations and inside these stations. It was a part of the scene.
Anybody who thinks otherwise was not there. Certainly

dope was a central element of the youth culture. Shit, it permeated all aspects of it.

Frank Wood: Drugs played a huge part at these stations. The proliferation of cannabis was all part of it. You couldn't separate the two. That is, the music and the fan, and the music was about getting high. I knew of stations run by junkies. There was an "us versus them" feeling. Some people in underground radio ended up addicts, and no doubt many members of the audience already were.

Roland Jacopetti: There was certainly a lot of dope smoked in and around KSAN during those years, but I seldom worked stoned because it would cause me to make technical errors and the deadlines were too tight. It took me a while to get comfortable around all this, but eventually I was.

Tim Powell: Dope was not a big item at the stations I worked for. That is, it wasn't smoked on the premises all that much. When it was smoked, it was usually in the still of the night when the buildings had no other tenants in them and everything was locked up. In the 1970s I visited KMET in LA and was shown a special room that was built which separated two record libraries. The small room had its own ventilation duct. I was told that the former general manager had built this room especially for the smoking of dope by the air staff and guests.

Stefan Ponek: Drugs were a shared experience at undergrounds. It formed a sort of brotherhood. We knew we could trust fellow participants. It's been a zillion years since I took acid, but I can remember being really "sure" about things back then, like whether a record was really good or sucked. The musicians that were around were really "heads," too. You could travel around the station or out on the street buzzed, and you knew who else was stoned. When your eyes met, BAM . . . you both knew, and it was magic. We were convinced back then that if the President got stoned he'd call off the war.

Ed Shane: Drugs definitely contributed to the scene at underground stations, but in a secondary way, not primary. Drugs might have made the music seem louder. They might have made music badly played less noticeable. The primary aspect of the drug culture as it affected commercial underground radio was the social nature of drug use.

Marijuana was an aperitif that loosened the party and brought dissimilar people into the same "club." It created "specialness" that gave its users a sense of belonging to something. That it was against the law even enhanced the idea, since the social fabric was woven by an illicit, yet seemingly harmless, ritual.

John Gehron: Drugs added a madcap aspect to an already zany environment at underground stations. They inspired the nude waterbed parties and over-the-top behavior that took place.

Larry Miller: Pot and other drugs of choice loosened things up. Drugs, at the time, were becoming more widely accepted, not so much a taboo. Marijuana was no longer perceived as such a big threat, except kids in the suburbs were beginning to turn on to heroin. We on the radio provided the soundtrack to the Big Movie, but it didn't always have a happy ending. Too many of us died.

Ben Fong-Torres: Some deejays were busted on the air for pot use.

Scoop Nisker: Yeah, jocks talked a lot about drugs on the air and even made a point of letting their audience know they were doing a joint at that very moment.

Bonnie Simmons: We were doing different drugs than the Top 40 deejays. Keep in mind that underground stations weren't alone in the use of drugs, and the drugs we used were psychedelics and pot not hardcore stuff, like heroin.

Raechel Donahue: We rarely played drugs on the air. That's my rather flippant response to the question about drug use in underground radio. One gets the impression that the world thought these stations were one big, continuous drug party. Sure, drugs were a pretty central element in the daily life of many underground stations, but not to the extent that it has been portrayed. I mean, it wasn't necessarily a destructive thing.

Tim Powell: Drugs provided us with a language. LSD was a popular drug of the day, and dosages were supposedly measured in "micrograms" or "mics." I used to say "KMPX, at 106 point 9 'mics,' " which was two codes in one. The other being a sexual innuendo—69. "Kilo-Mother-Pot-Xray" was also used in reference to KMPX for pretty obvious reasons. I used to explain my first name thusly: "Timothy as in Leary." One day Larry Miller pointed out that my last named rhymed with "bowel," so coming from where we were coming from, I referred to my program as "The Powell Movement on Wonderful Wadio Wabbex," or whatever.

Larry Miller: Drugs were perceived as a means of reaching a transcendental state. If that state was not achieved through meditation, à la Zen or yoga, then we smoked pot. Many of us also experimented with prescription drugs, like speed or downers, but cocaine hadn't really caught on yet, and heroin was still down the road. In our naive way, we used drugs to get closer to what we were doing on the air, not to become fiends.

Signs on studio walls:

>"Acid is groovy.
>Kill the pigs!"
>>and
>"Peace through Pot."

NOTES

1. John Kenneth Galbraith, *The New Industrial State* (New York: Signet Books, 1967), p. 218.

2. Abbie Hoffman, *Soon to Be a Major Motion Picture* (New York: Perigee Books, 1980), p. 113.

3. Jim Ladd, *Radio Waves* (New York: St. Martin's Press, 1991), p. 51.

4. Scoop Nisker, *If You Don't Like the News—Go Out and Make Some of Your Own* (Berkeley, CA: Ten Speed Press, 1994), p. 50.

5. Ibid., p. 62.

6. Jon Pareles, "Talkin' 'bout Two Generations," *New York Times*, May 5, 1996, p. 1.

7. Lewis Yablonsky, *The Hippie Trip* (New York: Pegasus Publishing, 1968), p. 241.

Chapter Six

A Long Strange Trip

It was all about money after Woodstock.
                              —Bill Graham

Rock and Roll music is higher than rebellion.
                              —Peter Townshend

Tom Wolfe characterized the transition from the 1960s to the years that followed as the move from the "we" to the "me" generation. Communal spirit was eventually supplanted by the corporate climber—"greed is good"—mentality. Psychedelically painted VW buses were traded in for slick, expensive status symbols. It became nirvana to drive a BMW. Noted one self-admitted former hippie, photographer Lee Nadel, "We dumped our bug for a beemer." Baby boomers were turning in their beads and lava lamps for hot tubs and polyester leisure suits. The civic fires were fading to flickering embers. The war in Vietnam was winding down, and inner cities were slipping into what would be a long period of complacency and decay. Protesters were abandoning their peace signs and placards.

The counterculture movement was getting long in the tooth, and many of its members were embracing more mainstream and traditional goals and aspirations, if not values. The pot and laced brownies of the flower child were replaced by the crack and heroin poison of armed dealers and pushers. For many, it was a good time to finally grow up and assume the mantle of adult responsibility. The anger and altruism inherent in rock music for nearly a decade bowed to the jejune patter and rhythms of disco and new wave—"corporate rock." Underground radio became a thing of the past as the baby boomer sought a less uncertain and chaotic future, taking refuge in that once unsavory realm known as the "material" world. Had we come full circle, many wondered, including writer Richard Goldstein:

> There were other . . . reminders that the counterculture bubble was about to burst. The promise of rock music—its vision of a multiracial community of the young—has been subverted by a record industry bloated on profit. The same entrepreneurial feeding frenzy has reduced the psychedelic experience to dayglo chatchkas, while its gurus scurried for the shelter of the wealth, remote from the battle-grounds of civil rights and Vietnam. Our faith in individualism was proving to be the ultimate marketable commodity. . . . With the rise of Nixon's silent majority, the counterculture fell into a numb silence.[1]

Reminiscing about underground radio prior to its co-optation by the mainstream, the editor of *Spin* magazine, Bob Guccione, Jr., observed in the *Los Angeles Times:*

> In 1969, FM radio was virtually underground. Innovative rock 'n' roll found a welcome there and settled into its new, and to begin with, barren homeland. In '71, FM radio was still fresh, experimental, gushingly enthusiastic, naive and fantastic. Every day, FM radio ran out of hours, not music. I'm not talking about today's classic rock, which is virtually just reheated AM radio, the silt of a great musical era. I'm talking about a spirit of musical diversity that was doomed as soon as the culture's commercial value could be accurately ascertained. Because once radio stations became hot properties, they sold for ever larger rices, and their owners became proportionately conservative to the size of their debts. I used to listen to Allison Steele on WNEW, New York's legendary FM station. She called herself the "Night Bird." She came on at midnight, read a different poem every night and talked for the first 15 minutes of her show before she played her first song. The mystical Zac on rival WPLJ was radio's Marlin, and WNEW's Jonathan Schwartz was FM's preeminent philosopher. In L.A., it was KMET that played the same pioneering music and shaped pop culture. The early DJ's were passionate and as wide-eyed as their invisible audiences about this new music and unfolding society. Once, I tuned Schwartz's show as he was asking listeners to tell him whether he should play Sinatra along with, say, King Crimson. The listeners voted yes. It was all that open then.[2]

Lamented media observer Joshua Mills in a recent commentary in the *New York Times:*

Twenty-five years later, where are the visionaries? Industry executives and consultants will tell you that creativity still exists, but in the hands of one program director. Yet in this potentially most diverse of media— the New York metropolitan listening audience, for example, has more than six dozen radio signals to choose among—there is little room on commercial radio for program hosts to express individuality. They have been transformed into precisely what their nickname of the 1950's denotes: Disk jockeys, riding hardware and preselected formulas, hanging on for dear life.[3]

A survey of published perspectives and conventional wisdom on the 1960s and 1970s, and on the underground radio phenomenon itself, reveals that numerous factors came into play—factors that ultimately contributed to the format's swift fade from the airwaves.

At the start of 1970, a *Life* magazine poll conducted by Louis Harris showed "a surprising feeling of tolerance and contentment"[4] among most Americans. The turbulence of the last few years seemed to be subsiding. Noted Fornatale and Mills, "The pendulum already had begun to swing: the tides of conservatism were washing over progressive FM, brushing away some of the sand castles that had been built."[5]

Former KSAN deejay Ben Fong-Torres observed in 1970:

It appears "underground radio," under the repressive nursing of net-work and/or corporate owners, is becoming just another spinoff of commercial, format radio. Top 40, middle-of-the-road, classical, coun-try, R&B, and, now, "underground." In short, underground radio is safe stuff nowadays, no more "progressive" in terms of hard politics, experimentation with music, or communication with the so-called "alternative" culture than the everyday AM station.[6]

The erosion in the numbers of underground outlets began early in the 1970s. For many listeners, the format was losing its pertinence to their everyday lives. According to Annie Gottlieb, the growing mind-set of the period took the baby-boomer generation in another direction, one that led it away from the 1960s message of underground radio. After 1970 the "movement" turned inward, Gottlieb argues, "which marked the beginning of the 'me' decade" and "the reemergent selfishness of the middle class."[7]

Reflecting on the evolving social environment, undergrounder Tom O'Hair remarked in a 1972 interview in *Variety* magazine: "If KSAN and other successful underground stations have changed . . . it's because 'soci-ety' has changed since '68 and '69."[8] O'Hair went on to comment that underground radio in the 1970s had become less political and more broad in its appeal to reflect that change.

The tide had shifted from the old underground rallying call of "Together we stand" to the mantra of the new gestalt—"Take care of number one." "By the end of 1970, the high tide of campus rebellion had receded, the Western democracies were back to business-as-usual," wrote David Caute,[9] echoing views espoused by Theodore Roszak many years earlier:

> Their communities have nevertheless become a market more and more dominated by hard-nosed entrepreneurial interests that have about as much concern for expanding consciousness as Al Capone had for arranging Dionysian festivals.[10]

In a 1972 interview with ABC-FM Radio president Allen Shaw, journalist Rex Weiner asked a question about the existing state of the underground medium which, in itself, summarized a scenario that many felt had led to the genre's premature descent. "Will 'PLJ follow the recurrent pattern of hip radio stations that start off well, become successful, then tighten up into a slick formula format, having gained a listenership with their original energy?" Weiner inquired. Shaw's response was that changing times demand changes, and ABC-FM was always thinking "progressively."[11]

Larry Yurdin, who had pioneered freeform radio years before it had manifested in commercial underground, hoped to prevent the dissipation of alternative media. In 1970 he led the first Alternative Media Conference and advocated that in addition to playing the right music, these stations "must be for the people, must be controversial, must be a link between the people and what is going on."[12] His challenge was to be embraced by fewer and fewer commercial broadcasters.

In her insightful and comprehensive organizational analysis of KMPX and KSAN, Susan Krieger writes that the stations' staff (Donahue's gang) was, from the start, at odds with management, which desired more professionalism as a means of generating more income. Ultimately, at KSAN in the late 1960s, management began to broaden the station's appeal to make this happen. It was management's contention that the station had to be less exclusive in its programming if it were to grow. Krieger cites a disgruntled staffer's reaction to this unhappy turn of direction. Complains Ed Bear, "Freeform radio is being absorbed into the lukewarm goo of commercial compromise."[13]

In Krieger's view, "The dilemma of cooptation is a moral one. When people of the radio station worry about being coopted, they worry about

WABX-FM deejays appear on public television in 1969. From left to right: Larry Miller, Dave Dixon, Jim Hampton, Dan Carlisle, and Jerry Lubin.

becoming corrupt, going bad, selling their souls as they sell their time." She concedes, however, that "there is no alternative if the station is to survive than for it to change in such ways as will allow an increasing integration with a larger society."14

> *Dusty Street:* Everybody has to survive, even radio stations. But when the corporations and owners took over, that was really the end of our brand of radio.

> *Dave Dixon:* Greed killed it. We were doing great with local sponsorships, but management wanted national business, and that was anathema to our sound. The national tapes were in stark contrast to WABX's sound. They compromised our integrity and credibility.

> *Raechel Donahue:* Big business folded the tribe's tent. In the independent radio world, management evolved from the talent pool, but corporate radio drew from the primordial slime in the shallower pool of sales. Pretty soon it was only numbers that mattered and especially the ones with the dollar signs in front of them.

> *Ed Shane:* Success killed it. Underground radio went from being a very special entity, enjoyed like a private and exclusive club, to being everyone's radio. The more popular it became, the less exclusive it seemed, the less "mystique" it possessed.

> *John Gehron:* The decline came with the success of the FM band to attract listeners, the owners reclaiming control of their stations to reach this audience for advertisers, AOR [album-oriented rock] replacing its structurelessness, the changing attitudes against drugs, and the baby boomers maturing to the next level of life. As we moved out of the period, the music was being reclaimed and controlled by the labels, just as the owners were taking back their stations to turn losses into profits. Their AM stations were losing listeners and revenue, and they turned to FM to make up the losses. At the same time, society's tastes began to fragment and there were not enough AM stations for the new formats that were developing to reach these audience segments.

> *Allen Shaw:* Ironically, even at its height, the actual audience share of freeform underground stations was marginal. The commercial potential of underground radio

proved to be illusory in the end. It was only partially finan-cially viable for about four years, a shorter run than "Mod Squad" had on ABC television.

Dwight Douglas: What occurred after the ratings didn't match the investments in new staffs. Something had to be done. A format had to be implemented. The quote from ABC-FM—"We can no longer let the inmates run the asy-lum"—meant that every PD had to break the news to the deejays that they would no longer program their own music. Some quit. Some protested, but most didn't want to give up the big money. Some blossomed under this new format approach that wasn't supposed to sound like a format, and more and more Top 40 deejays came over to play the music they personally liked. First off, undergrounds went away because they were more experimental than good. Wretched excess—too much Jim Laddism. Talk, talk, talk! Nixon goes down in '72, and some deejay wouldn't let it be. Next, pushing the musical envelope outside of the desires and frame of reference of the audience. But the next important element was competition. Formatted FM with better sales staffs suffocated these mom and pop operators. Even Metromedia and ABC-FM freeforms lost to stations doing formats.

Bonnie Simmons: What success we had spawned a flock of imitators. The competition hurt individual revenues. Sta-tions like KMEL had huge budgets, so it had to make a dollar to be viable. These stations, like any other, were expected to make money by the corporations which owned them, especially when ratings went up. You can well imagine that all this had a less than beneficial impact on programming.

Writing in *Rolling Stone*, Ben Fong-Torres concurred with his former colleague's assessment:

As FM rock became a money-maker, KSAN drew increasingly pow-erful competition, and as the booming record industry began to frag-ment into disco, punk, funk, and other responses to what was called "corporate rock," KSAN's policy of letting DJs choose the music began to backfire. The sound, to put it simply, became inconsistent.[15]

Larry Miller: The transition into commercially successful "progressive" and then to AOR meant that we had to leave out the other stuff and concentrate on rock. If there was only one FM station in a market doing the format, then there wasn't much pressure, but as soon as there was another station competing, then the choices began to tighten up. By '72, we were using categories and sequences or clocks. By 1980, we were using very tight clocks, and by 1990, we were preprogramming the music. I should say they, because by that time I was long gone from rock radio and had returned to classical. To cut to the chase, what killed creative alternative radio was the return to Top 40. We thought we had conquered the beast, but it snuck back on us in the form of disco formats on FM in the late 1970s. Mencken said that "no one ever went broke underestimating the taste of the American public," and he was right. Lowest common denominator programming, play the hits, one cut per album. All the mechanics and style of Top 40 came back in the guise of Contemptible Hit Radio (CHR).

John Gorman: The subculture was co-opted by the mainstream, as were the underground stations. In the end, radio was real estate.

Roland Jacopetti: KSFX was an early attempt by commercial media to mine the counterculture, and it was a dismal failure. They just didn't know how to do it; didn't know how to keep their hands out of it and leave the creative decisions to creative people. It started out as an album rock station, hiring a number of KSAN people—Voco, Phil, Buchanan, and so forth. Tony Pigg worked there before we went back to New York. But there was always the sense of management deciding what music was to be played, when the breaks were to occur, when the spots were to run, and on and on. So one thing that happens in a situation like that is the jocks begin to resent the music because it's part of management's coercion, and then they begin to ignore the music. Broadcast carts came along to replace records. Of course, this becomes the kiss of death, because the jock loses touch with the album from which the carted cut originated. KSFX finally went Top 40, which by then wasn't much of a transition. All they had to do was fire the existing deejays and hire a bunch of burned out Top 40 jocks. After a few years things got dicey at KSAN, too. It became obvious that Metromedia was lots more interested in the station than it had been. By the

1970s, it was in fancy new digs and had a new general manager. Tom Donahue had gotten back in the driver's seat for a while but then dropped dead. The true punctuation mark, I guess. Jerry Graham became Metromedia's new man. He was a guy who didn't know a radio from a Waring blender, but he knew the corporate walk and talk. He was very genial, but I didn't trust him. I thought he was the kind of guy who would call the corporate office at the slightest sign of a problem. Well, eventually, I was gone, and, as they say, "out of sight, out of mind." I heard through the grapevine that the station began to decline, that it had lost much of its listenership.

Dwight Douglas: The day these FMs took advertising from the Army and the politicians was the beginning of the slide. This was the end of the idealism and the start of the thrust of big business. When a station like KDKB, which started as the dream of a couple of guys coming back from Woodstock, ended up being sold for many millions of dollars a decade later, it was very apparent what the whole thing had become. Most of the old hippies who owned those early stations sold out to large broadcast companies. Idealism in business is an oxymoron.

Dan Carlisle: Most of us knew that the survival of freeform underground required a left-of-center presentation. When it moved toward the middle ground, it lost its essence. When it became a cash cow, that was it.

Tim Powell: It became bad radio, thanks to a lot of bad managers. By "bad" I mean crappy, unlistenable, shitty. It is painful to admit how many bad months of crummy radio I've programmed because of an edict from a bad manager, or a whole stew of them. During 1967 to 1969, when the underground thing was at its zenith, there were some good radio stations with horrid GMs. That's because they kept the hell out of the way, like the manager at WABX, who let the programmers do what they were paid to do. Many of the early managers in FM rock were rejects from AM. My first GM reportedly returned to Michigan and his old, pre-radio line of work. Aluminum siding salesman. Cross my heart.

Russ Gibb: Underground radio just didn't grow. We didn't change or evolve. We were static on FM. We wanted it to be 1968 forever. What was once cutting-edge radio became a caricature of its former self. It was no longer good radio.

Kate Ingram: Bad radio is when the programming is directed to the lowest common denominator, and that is what eventually happened in commercial underground because management wanted the big payoff.

Tim Powell: They got the big payoff, and we got the big fuck-off, but the environment was in league with the profit-seekers. There was much less interest in quality and much more interest in quantity of profit. For example, the record companies released too much marginal product. The free-form stations played too much of it, while the evolving formatted FM rockers stuck with Zeppelin, the Stones, the Moody Blues, and Crosby, Stills, and Nash, and creamed the freeformers, who played the newest but not the best.

The underground format was not without its outside critics as well. Among those who felt it failed to live up to its original promise of innovation and creativity were rock performers such as Harry Nilsson, who assessed the state of its programming approach as such:

For one thing, the sound is monotonous. After a little while, all the music sounds the same. It's too categorized. The people who run these stations are a lot less liberal than they think they are. They seem to have a phobia against any record that has become successful on AM. Secondly, the music seems to be standardized into a mixture of rock and blues, and every song seems to have a downer viewpoint. I don't seem to hear much happy music. I seem to be hearing blues, blues, and more blues to the point where I now identify freeform stations with the blues. . . . One of my biggest objections is the tone of the programs. They're so serious, too serious for my taste. After all, radio is a form of entertainment.[16]

Dave Pierce: Well, that's eventually how it was seen by its managers, as an entertainment product. The rock artists became mainstream celebrities, too. That is when the lobotomy to AOR or to psuedo-underground took place.

Pierce's opinion was reflected in a statement by Bill Greeley in a 1970 article in *Variety:*

WCBS-FM, which would like to mine the new radioland, runs fullpage poster ads in *FM Guide* with the slogan "Right on," but it is about as right-on as the Edsel. And it should be pointed out that WOR-FM, a formula rocker, is more underground in its commercials than programming.[17]

Pierce's point on the sellout of rock artists is also evident in a cogent examination of the recording industry, *Rockonomics: The Money Behind the Music*, by Marc Eliot, who assesses the influence of commercialization on rock and roll performers:

> Rock stars no longer symbolized the rock counterculture. They were, instead, the very icons of material extravagance; their self-indulgent music, dress and style of living was in marked contrast to the mass audience they no longer cared to represent. Lyrics preached passivity and conformity rather than assertive individuality. The romantic ideal reverted to the courtly syrup of pre-rock pop.[18]

Tim Powell: They took this pap and playlisted it on their prefab rock stations. Lee Abrams did it. Actually, the old formula, established hype came back with Allen Shaw and Bob Henabery. They brought "the Monster that Killed the Grooviness Forever" to the airwaves. It just took ABC-FM and eventually Lee Abrams to give the format the coup de grâce. CBS-FM's "Mellow" and Abrams' "Superstars" helped rot the corpse.

Ed Shane: When Lee Abrams put formula to the underground and developed the "Superstars" format, many stations adopted it. The approach found a willing and enthusiastic market. Stations that had been underground or freeform could not compete directly with the new entries without being accused of "selling out"—that is, sounding too commercial, minimizing the risk, playing just the hits, and so on. The problem with the revolutionaries is that they don't want to win the war; they'd rather fight the battles. Few from early underground radio understood that the rise of the highly commercial "Superstars" or album-oriented rock format was a true victory for the pioneers, who tried to create something new in the late 1960s and early 1970s.

John Gehron: Lee Abrams took a lot of early heat as a proponent of this approach and developed the AOR format. Some held out for the pure approach but soon were overshadowed by the AOR stations in ratings and revenue. There are few remnants of those stations today—WXRT, KINK, and WNEW-FM. All others were swept away as owners began maximizing their investment. In fact, the growth of FM, which was started by progressive/underground radio, caused its own demise. With more people using the FM band, owners started trying other formats. When WOR in New York went Top 40 on FM, people said it wouldn't work and that it destroyed everything that FM stood for. But it was a success. In Philadelphia in 1970, I did oldies on FM; again they said it wouldn't work, but it was a huge success, so much so that in 1972, I was asked to change progressive WCBS-FM to oldies. It quickly became the most listened to FM in America.

Media critics found both positive and negative things to report about the metamorphosis that was taking place in underground radio in the early 1970s. On the revamping of ABC's "Love" format, an alternative publication, *Zygote*, felt that the change was more than justifiable. "Music programming was better elsewhere and the 'philosophy' involved was too syrupy, not to mention insultingly banal. Nobody was listening, and for good reason."[19]

Concomitantly, the *Atlantic Newsletter* praised the efforts of the ABC-FM chain of radio stations for bringing album music programming to the airwaves:

The ABC-FM chain is really doing some nice progressive radio across the country. The have hired some of the best veteran progressive music freaks from various parts of the country—J.J. Jackson, Michael Cuscuna, Tony Pigg, Dave Herman, Vin Scelsa, Mike Turner, Larry Miller, Jerry Lubin, etc. It looks like ABC is doing to progressive what Kinney has done to the record business, taking the best and consolidating it. This huge establishment is really behind this progressive trip, and as long as the deejays have as much freedom as they presently possess, it should turn out to be some of the best radio in the country.[20]

In 1973 *Broadcasting* magazine extolled ABC-FM for its cultivation and honing of the format. "The ABC-FM group of stations in many ways legitimized the move of progressive rock to a more structured form."[21] The article was entitled "Progressive Rock: A little older, a little wiser, a little more structured. FM wild child of the late sixties matures into a still distinct but more disciplined format."

Lee Abrams: It was better radio—"professional" radio. The tightening that took place was necessary to make it more broadly appealing and financially viable. There was too much belief that the jocks knew more than the listeners, and they frequently dictated the wrong mix of music. Stations were more interested in preaching their brand of lifestyle than reaching out to the "people."

Dwight Douglas: The formatted, tighter, more focused operations suffocated the mom and pop operators. Even Metromedia and ABC freeform stations lost out to those with clearly defined and executed formats. That's why they made their own adjustments. By 1975, AOR music was a large enough library to support a whole format of quality rock without folk, jazz, and avant garde approaches.

Al Wilson: As competition heated up in the radio marketplace, the move to research became necessary. Believe it or not, the advent of consumer-based research heralded the disappearance of underground radio. It dispelled the notion that we were educating the audience, as opposed to reflecting what it wanted, by researching and testing music and listening habits before airing songs. Research taught us that we didn't know everything we thought we knew.

Tim Powell: That's what it came down to—numbers, charts, and graphs. Due to the size of the business, everything has to be formula-"ized." It is my experience that when ephemerals like "bullets" on the *Billboard* chart mean something—then the real meaning is lost.

The Federal Communications Commission, too, was having a chilling effect on these stations. In an interview with ABC's Allen Shaw, the *Village Voice* noted that the feds had

> handed down a ruling involving a Des Moines, Iowa, "freeform" radio station, issuing an edict that a freeform radio format "gives the announcer such control over the records to be played that it is inconsistent with the strict controls that the license must exercise to avoid questionable practices."[22]

Acknowledging the impact of the commission's actions, Shaw responded by saying:

The network is constantly tightening up on its controls over the announcer. We used to give them a lot more freedom, but now we are out of the freeform business entirely . . . I agree in full with the FCC that freeform stations are not desirable.[23]

In an interview in *Walrus* a month later, Shaw claimed that the Commission's activities had not influenced programming decisions at the network:

The FCC ruling was something that was hardly mentioned around management circles here and no one, and this is the absolute fact, no one above me, ever said one word to me about that statement by the FCC regarding freeform radio. No one ever even mentioned it.[24]

Word had, in fact, circulated among radio executives' offices well over a year before Shaw's statement that the commission was quite concerned with the message broadcast by many underground stations, in particular as found in the lyrics of the rock music they aired. The FCC cited "drug oriented" song lyrics as a violation of licensees' public trust. Wrote John J. O'Connor in the *Wall Street Journal:* "There are the establishment critics understandably nervous about certain aspects of the new subculture. Earlier this year one FCC Commissioner suggested in a speech that radio stations playing certain rock records . . . should not have their licenses renewed."[25]

Robert Hilliard: Many stations used the FCC as a scapegoat—to alibi their own inability to manage their on-air personnel or to obfuscate their deliberate appeal to prurient interests to hype ratings and, of course, ad revenue. The FCC was, in fact, pretty laid back about content during that period. It did express concern when station management did not live up to its obligation to control its own programming.

Charles Laquidara: There was plenty of tension. As a matter of fact, WBCN had filed a lawsuit back in the early seventies to try to force the FCC to make a ruling on obscenity in music as an art form. John Lennon's "Working Class Hero" was the test case. The commission declined to take part in the case.

Reacting, at least in part, to the stir coming from Washington, WPLJ-FM implemented a daily music playlist in August 1971, referring to it as a "program aid" in a memo to the air staff. "As the use of these aids develops you should expect some refinements and alterations from time to time," stated the station's program director, Mitchell Weiss.[26]

Conceded Shaw in the *Walrus* interview:

> I do have suspicion based upon hearsay that virtually every progressive rock operator of any importance, which would also include Metromedia, and I suppose the Century Group, KSHE and WABX, and maybe even WBCN in Boston, are [*sic*] reevaluating their position in the markets they are in.[27]

Dave Pierce: The fix was in on a number of levels. As they say, the fort was being charged from all directions.

Dave Dixon: Management was insensitive to what they were doing. In fact, to be truthful, they treated people like used tissue. To hell with things like integrity and creative freedom. Protect your little money-maker at all costs. The bodies began piling up.

John Gehron: As I've already stated, there was as much undoing from the inside as from management and other external forces. All managers were not devoid of an understanding and appreciation of what freeform/underground radio had contributed.

Dan Carlisle: Certainly drugs can't be ruled out as a contributing agent in the decline of this format. There was a lot of that going on. Still, I believe the most damaging event was the rise in power of the sales department and the takeover by management.

Roland Jacopetti: Well, there's always the drug thing, but the arrogance and elitism probably did a bigger number on underground. KSAN had acquired a real reputation in this area, but it wasn't without some justification. What had been happening was unique and in some ways exceptional.

Charles Laquidara: I guess there were a lot of egos out there, just as there are in every field of art and entertainment. Does that detract from the product or the message? I don't think so. I can hate Frank Sinatra and Al Capp, and all they stood for, but still appreciate and learn from their work. The format died because the establishment co-opted it when it noticed, and correctly so, that this music

Tom and Raechel Donahue in the early days of the long strange trip.

and attitude was a money-maker. That's when it metamorphosized into AOR—the big-business format.

Lee Abrams: The rampant elitism of the staffs of underground outlets killed them. I saw cases where stations refused to play Led Zeppelin after they became widely known because they were too popular. Tremendous biases and prejudices existed which accelerated their fall from grace.

Dave Pierce: You can blame it on a lot of things, but the simple truth is times change. Things don't stay the same, no matter how good they are perceived. The clock ticks and things either evolve or erode. The seventies left us behind. The revolution was over. Underground was obsolete. Nobody cared anymore. Corporate America regained control of the few isolated stations that had gotten loose. In my book, *The Disc Jockeys*, I give a personal account of how we did it to ourselves at KMPX and KPPC. It's a sad and glorious momento mori.

Stefan Ponek: Sometimes I wonder if the whole period was just a wonderful weird dream fantasy that we just had to grow out of. What's strange is that so many of us had the same dream.

Raechel Donahue: It was a great party, but it's always important to know when to go home. I didn't want to be the last one to leave.

Bonnie Simmons: I don't think we need to eulogize it. Nothing really ruined it. It just went its natural course.

Scoop Nisker: I'd agree. In my book I say "Freeform FM radio had turned into little more than a top forty format for the flower children who had, for the most part, joined the economic rat race of the Reagan years."

BLOWIN' IN THE WIND

Quod di omen avertant. (May the gods avert this omen.)

—Cicero

The following memorandum sent by WPLO program director Ed Shane to the station's programming staff in the late 1970s, served as a sign that change was, indeed, blowin' in the wind.

Tom Donahue's KMPX/KSAN team gather for a group photo. Some of those present would go on to fame in other media, such as television. Note, for example, sitcom star Howard Hesseman in the top left hand corner. A few years down the line he would be portraying Dr. Johnny Fever, a whacked out deejay on "WKRP in Cincinnati."

Some random thoughts on hearing the Overture from "Tommy" and "In A Gaddada Vida" on the station in the same half hour segment.

First, enjoyable.

Second, I wonder if the 1968 feel should not stay with a rock station. What we have basically is the rock sound, while today's music seems to be shying away from basic beat rock.

To my way of thinking, 1958 and 1968 were the best years that rock ever had. Chuck Berry, the Monotones, Jackie Wilson, Buddy Holly, the Big Bopper, the Drifters. More, of course. They got it all together in 1958 and started rock on its way. Sure there had been practitioners earlier than these artists but none had been accepted at the level of these people.

1968 was the same way. Hendrix, Cream, Butterfly, and on and on. Why should these people not be recognized on a regular basis by a contemporary station?

The New Seekers record is great. But is it rock? I'm not saying that it should not be played, just that there should be balance. There are some fine modern (1970) rock pieces, of course. These should be our concentration. But with a great number of New Seekers sounds dominating the record market today, maybe older rock is the answer.

Right now there are no particular trends. We seem to be waiting musically for another Bill Haley, Chuck Berry, Elvis Presley, Beatles, Stones, Jefferson Airplane, Cream, and Hendrix. Until he, she or they come . . . what? Founder in the abyss of New Seekers and Elephant's Memory? I say no.

To state this another way. I'm not saying abandon all modern material. Nor am I saying to overlook years other than 1958 or 1968. It's "sound" we're after. A listener should be able to turn on WPLO-FM or a similar station and say immediately "That's PLO-FM," "That's a rock station," or "That's a progressive station."

LONG AGO AND "FAR OUT!"

Tinsel reflect / electrical speck
Glossy pink shadow / Titanic bulk wreck

—M. C. Keith

The following unique and contrasting retrospectives (one by Stefan Ponek, from the station staff level; the other by Allen Shaw, from the network executive level) describe the period in which the underground radio genre and the nation were undergoing a significant seismic transformation in their political and cultural behavior, mood, and orientation.

Stefan Ponek: It's not so much a need to eulogize under-ground/freeform radio as it is a desire to recall it so as not to lose what it meant—what its value was. I was looking through Todd Gitlin's sixties book the other day. Besides showing me I had a crappy memory, I came away with a clear notion that Gitlin and we KSANers were more inter-ested in a self-justifying kind of "he said, she said"—as though anybody really cared. I felt Gitlin's trip was more an inventory of himself in an attempt to make sense of his own long trip, and I found that an easy sort of "need" to identify with. Our real experience was of depth, and all the things that didn't get remembered were dropped just because not enough people were there to share the experience. The era was a state of mind rather than the sum of its events, and it applied to all events and situations, and it's still hanging out latent in a lot of fifty-year-olds these days. But none of us want to look like those aging jazz buffs of the last couple of decades, using jive talk that didn't work anymore, wearing their stupid twirly mustaches, drink-ing too much and pretending they were the only ones who really understood what Monk was playing. Yet that's ex-actly who we are—updated. Frightening. The Diggers and Wavy Gravy personify it. They made the really scary into a big cosmic joke. Which was the only truth. It was a time when we really needed some cosmic truth. The world could blow up any second, yet we had the resources to live without poverty, disease, or overpopulation. So we thought. Even though Tim Leary took himself a little too seriously after a while, he had still been right. Everything we had known had suddenly become unnecessary, just use-less structure that needed discarding. We learned too much too fast, in a spiritual sense (common among relig-ious students, I hear). We got the knowledge that the world could really be a simple good place but didn't get the wisdom of how slowly things really change. War was only serving the needs of the military-industrial complex, not the people. There is an argument for the need to keep people employed and searching for answers with that system, but let's try to stay above it. For all the pragmatists among us, and we broadcasters were operating on our pragmatic, commercial interests primarily, we all were tuning into the spiritual questioning with a kind of hope that wasn't always tempered by reserve or deep judgment (the styles re-flected that). We were in a hurry because it seemed so really possible and necessary after all [we] had done. World War II, space exploration, birth control, vaccines, public works, ad infinitum. All this and the power to destroy the world in an instant gave urgency to a new way of seeing the whole thing. It didn't seem naive considering the emergency we felt. The world had gotten this way really fast! You didn't have to be a hippie or a college radical to appreciate this. And it wasn't long before the established methods of dialogue for change appeared ludicrous to anyone. This is where there was hope for radio. It made it worth exploring the format that followed this drumbeat. It was a growing sentiment. It had commercial potential! Nixonian-style self-interest was embedded in our institutions, so trashing the "system" was a constructive move, we thought, and it scared the shit out of those with a lot to lose. Those of us with nothing to lose could enjoy it with great glee. It was not lost on us that our stations were owned and regulated by those with something to lose. We proceeded for a while as if we didn't really care. Placating these powers-that-be became an art form in itself. This was one of Tom Donahue's great strengths. He had a way of ducking for the sidelines when the going got hot. However, one of those times was when he stepped down as program director. I stepped in only to have to face such things as the legalities of our announcing political rally demonstrations and the intrusion of U.S. Treasury agents into our station. They were demanding that we take action against one of our more racially minded deejays for allegedly threatening the life of the president. David Hilliard had suggested in a speech that people ought to try and kill Nixon, and he was arrested for it. In support of Hilliard, a Black Panther member, our black deejay, Roland Young, suggested that his audience could show their support by sending Nixon a similar note. It also became necessary to remind jocks to stay with more commercial music, that they worked at a property owned by the establishment and regulated by the government, and they could not risk the owner's investment in the interest of their own political agendas without losing their jobs. Donahue had side-stepped that phase. Just before he died, we were face to face with the final commercial battles, playlisting and commercialism, and his death loosely marks the birth of what later was labeled "AOR" programming. It was the ultimate mutation of the original "ugly-radio" Top 40 thing.

Donahue sidestepped that too. Full circle and off the merry-go-round! It was also at this time that radio began to pull away from movement politics, and the stylistic backlash into the disco era began. Those of us so intensely involved with the late sixties radio era had a lot of weird things happen to us in the late seventies. Those who stayed hip and into drugs went to cocaine and its eventual nose-dive. Some adapted to disco—I'm reminded of the Johnny Fever goes disco episodes on "WKRP in Cincinnati." Others, like myself, moved into other directions, and for another decade, I wasn't really sure of what the hell had happened, but I knew it was intense and important. Vietnam vets were coming home, with their demons and doubts. There was a feeling of dragging something heavy along behind me into my new ventures. For some, there was a postpartum to the sixties that left shame, fear, and rage in the dark recesses of their minds. A lot of quiet healing is probably at the root of the whole "recovery" popularity of the eighties and nineties. Mercifully, the boomers are now headed to fight AARP's battles, and they are off the pages of *People* and *Time* at last.

Allen Shaw: There is something in the human spirit that passionately embraces freedom. Freedom of expression, especially in America, is a sacred right. When this right is threatened or challenged, it invariably produces a strong reaction from those sensing its potential demise. The idea of freeform/underground radio appealed to that part of our human spirit. But, as with American democracy itself, with freedom comes responsibility. Many of the station personnel I had so enthusiastically assembled to make real underground radio possible ended up abusing the freedom they were given. They smoked dope in the studio, said "shit" and "fuck" on the air, and paid little attention to what the audience they were there to serve might want them to do. They complained about the commercials we aired and asked for a raise in the same breath. I had become aware of the hypocrisy of what were largely middle- and upper-middle-class white kids who were used to enjoying the comforts of their affluent backgrounds but wanted to play in radio without any rules. The maintenance of the air staff became consuming. A big part of me was really committed to the political and social revolution of the time, but I was never really a hippie. I did not smoke dope, eat organic food, or live in a commune. At heart, I was a commercial broadcaster. I was very much aware of the realities I faced at ABC. We were a commercial enterprise. We were the company that spawned Dick Clark, Howard Cosell, Cousin Brucie, and the "Mod Squad." I felt immense internal pressure to deliver commercial success with the FM stations I had been entrusted with. Within the network during these years, there was a high degree of ambition to be the best within every medium. The AM stations were the most successful commonly owned group in the country. The ABC Radio networks were the most successful among all networks, and the ABC-TV network was beginning to reach parity with CBS and NBC in the ratings. I had never been second-guessed or restricted by my immediate boss, Hal Neal. I knew I had the support of Broadcast Division President Elton Rule. Leonard Goldenson, founder and chairman of ABC, was, quite frankly, far too decent a person and too supportive of our outrageous efforts in FM for me to disappoint. The questionable lyrics, the anti-Nixon and antiwar content of our programming was never censored or curtailed in any way by the ABC corporate brass, contrary to what most of the counterculture press believed. But making a profit on the considerable investment the company had now made in FM was something that would have to happen. By the summer of 1971, we had been doing the most freeform, unrestricted radio you could do in this country and still keep your FCC license. When the summer of 1971 Arbitron ratings came out for our seven markets, they showed that all of our stations were doing rather poorly. In fact, one full year of doing freeform commercial underground radio had produced audience levels that were not even as good as those we had when we were airing the "Love" format on a partially automated basis. The truth in America is that many sins will be forgiven if you are a winner. The unforgivable sin is losing. I know that I, and the company, could have tolerated all of the problems, controversies, and unorthodox personnel involved with freeform/underground radio, if the product had been capable of producing viable audiences and profits. However, that was not to be. The truth is that 96 percent of people listening to radio in 1971 chose not to listen to freeform/underground radio. Some of the independently owned underground FM stations could survive on a 2 [percent] share of the audience because their operating expenses were low. At ABC, we had the burden of union engineers, expensive real estate, and higher corporate expectations to contend with. All along, I had been encouraged by my associations at WABC-AM, the bastion of Top 40 success, to consider formatting album-oriented rock. Rick Sklar, operations director at WABC, and Julian Breen, its PD, had watched my struggle with freeform radio for a year or more. Breen said, "Allen, someday you know you'll have to go to a playlist." A playlist? A playlist to our deejays was like the cross to Dracula, but I knew deep in my heart that a playlist was inevitable. Bob Henabery, ABC-owned stations program director, had a keen personal interest in progressive rock music, and I sought his counsel. He suggested we get a box lunch and drive out to Jones Beach to blue-sky the potential of formatting this music. There we talked about the original way the music had been programmed on the "Love" format. That is, play only the best cuts from the best-selling albums. People don't lay out hard cash to buy a record album unless they really like it. WABC-AM had successfully used record sales as its primary information to determine what songs to play. The logic is hard to dispute. If this week, 56 million people lay out hard cash to buy the Moody Blues album and only 2 million buy the Buzzy Linhart album, which album should be given more exposure on the radio station? It is also true that on every album, there were usually three or four good cuts and seven or eight not so good cuts. Why would you want to play the not so good cuts when you could be playing one of the really good ones? I realized the time had come to apply these programming principles to FM progressive rock radio. Back in the office, Bob Henabery, WPLJ program director Mitch Weiss, and I spent hours crafting a system for selecting and mixing album rock music and defining a new style for our FM station disc jockeys. We categorized the music as follows: A—strongest cuts from current top-selling rock albums, often the hit single played on AM Top 40; B—other best cuts from current top-selling rock albums; C—strongest cuts from older top-selling rock albums; and D—other best cuts from older top-selling rock albums. We knew that our unique secret weapon against our freeform competitors, as well as the big Top 40 stations, was the "B" list. Here were the best cuts from the most popular current rock albums, other than the hit singles the

AM stations were playing, that the freeform stations rarely got around to airing. These were the "Babba O'Reillys," the "Tiny Dancers," and the "Whole Lotta Loves." The best of the best, and we would be the only stations playing them with any frequency. We decided the disc jockeys would eliminate all the informal, rambling chatter so prevalent on freeform FM stations. They would be upbeat but not as frenetic as AM Top 40 jocks, yet far more energized than the laid-back freeformers. Essentially, we were going to provide a rock music format that was positioned right in between AM Top 40 and freeform/underground FM. Our slogan for all seven stations was going to be "Rock 'n' Stereo." Hip? No! Commercial? Definitely! In September of 1971, Bob Henabery and I flew to all seven ABC-owned FM stations and presented the new format plans to each staff. As expected, many of the freeform disc jockeys were outraged, some storming out of the room with shouts of "I quit!" and "Capitalist pigs!" Some of the DJs resigned themselves to giving it a try until they could find another job. In two weeks flat, we had changed the formats of all seven stations just in time for the fall 1971 Arbitron (ARB in those days) rating sweep. Underground radio on ABC-FM was over. Upon listening to the new format on WPLJ in New York, I felt we were on to something big. It sounded so good. When the fall ratings results came out in January 1972, every single one of our seven stations made dramatic gains. The underground press, however, ran numerous lengthy accounts of the purge of freedom from ABC-FM. There were a lot of "We told you it wouldn't last at ABC" articles. But the validity of our decision was confirmed in the ratings reports. The people had voted for "Rock 'n' Stereo." I had not anticipated the shock waves our sweeping moves to a format would have on freeform/underground radio in other markets. Radio and record industry trade press called me for detailed reasoning behind our actions. Other FM station owners noticed our immediate success and began tightening up their music playlists and curbing the amount of talk their deejays could get away with. With the end of the Vietnam War and President Nixon's resignation, the mood of the nation was swinging away from the heavy negatives of the late 1960s and toward a much more active and positive place. It was a time for "Crocodile Rock" and "Silly Love Songs." Bands and performers like Foreigner, Elton John, Bad Company,

Rod Stewart, Peter Frampton, and Boston defined album rock of the mid-1970s. Our stations were playing the best cuts off these best albums. During the mid-1970s our ratings continued to grow. KLOS under program director Tom Yates, WRIF under program director Tom Bender, and WPLJ under Larry Berger became the top-rated FM stations in their markets and turned significant profits. In 1975, KLOS made $1 million profit. That year the FM station division was profitable as a whole. We were the most listened to group of FM stations in the country. In 1976, I was elected president of the ABC-owned FM stations. Some of our early programming personnel at the stations went on to spread the format into other markets as consultants in later years. Lee Abrams and Fred Jacobs from WRIF in Detroit, Dwight Douglas from WDVE in Pittsburgh, and Tom Yates from KLOS in Los Angeles were among them. WPLJ (under general managers Willard Lochridge and Nick Trigony), WRIF (with general managers Jack Minkow and Jay Hoker), and KLOS (under general managers John Winnaman and Bill Sommers) grew to be as profitable, and in some cases more profitable, than their AM sister stations. KLOS reached $10 million in annual profits in the early 1990s. Underground radio captured that part of all of us that cherishes raw freedom, believing in a cause, and playing without rules. That was the powerful genesis of that kind of radio. In the end, it did not last, not because anyone wanted it dead, but because the audience for it faded along with the emotions, events, and times that had given it life.

BACKS TO THE FUTURE

The sixties were good for America.

—Oliver Stone

Accept that which is already in you, and around you.

—Malcolm X

Anybody who listens to the radio now knows that it's strictly business, y'know.

—Frank Zappa

Can commercial underground radio enjoy a revival, a second coming? It left the airwaves nearly a quarter of a century ago, having been written off as an aberration and a failure by what the counterculture pejoratively called the corporate "pigs" and capitalist "suits" (devils in Brooks Brothers), if not by its deejays and programmers.

Scoop Nisker: I don't think anything similar to underground FM rock could happen unless new circumstances prevailed. Perhaps a new radio band will be discovered. Maybe a new revolution will arise. Possibly new and better psychedelics.

Tim Powell: As much as I'd like to think it could happen again, it would take a new band, a music that is unexploited that has an audience, and it would take a staff that may be impossible to assemble.

Ed Shane: It cannot come back as it was. In fact, it should not. The commercial underground format was a product of a unique alignment of demographics, technology, and politics. It was a format for its time, in its time. Now that time is past.

Charles Laquidara: Underground wasn't meant to be a success. Once it became a success it failed. So how is it going to happen again?

John Gehron: There's no chance of it happening again. The closest thing to it is the alternative music format, but it has quickly been co-opted and controlled by the labels, consultants, and owners.

Thom O'Hair: Will radio ever be as exciting as it was during this revolutionary period in our history? No, I think not. The conditions are not conducive for the freedom necessary to bring it back and to generate the excitement that existed on the FM dial back then. Many factors are against it. First, the cost of a license. Just like buying a house, the monthly payment kills you. The payment is so high you have to make money right away. Freeform radio is a risky business. Who knows what it would do in today's marketplace, and who would buy time on it to keep it alive? You'd have to charge a very high rate per spot. You couldn't count on the "street" or local advertisers to keep you going until the station built a reputation for effective ad value. When all is considered, I don't think any station owner today would take the risk needed to launch a new freeform outlet.

Bonnie Simmons: Yeah, I just don't know where a place may exist for underground stations today. The importance of "marketing" in everyone's lives today and the folksy approach of those stations make an awkward match.

John Gorman: Like I've already stated, radio is a real estate game. It's a high price commodity. It's not Goodwill Industry.

Frank Wood: I don't think you'll see anything like commercial underground for a while, if ever again. Station properties are too expensive. No owner is going to hand over their multimillion dollar frequency to a bunch of deejays. Radio as a pure art form, as opposed to commerce, wasn't concerned with ratings and audience size, which are everything today.

Lee Abrams: Underground radio as it existed in the 1960s will never return because that era was a powerful, flukish time. I think we should let it rest in peace. It was magical but practically a cultural accident. Too much stuff was crammed into a short period—drugs, war, assassinations, riots, new bands, moon landing, synthesizers, et cetera. I definitely see new formats emerging that are deeper and more sophisticated. There is a generation of people who are burnt out on "Freebird" and "Layla"! They will need their own format.

Tim Powell: I hope that 1997 finds the listening public tired of chortling sidekicks, titty humor, and secret code words that hide class division if not plain racial hatred. Oh, that the current age finds some programmers and/or owners who recall the true milieu of rock radio and that this fucking apartheid in music starts to end.

Russ Gibb: There's a possibility that an underground-style format may reemerge, but not in the same way as before. That radio was for then. There may be new variations on the classic, but it will be relative to the times as they are today.

Ben Fong-Torres: The format may come back. But in order to succeed, it would need to be completely freeform eclectic, not any kind of permutation . . . not coalesced.

Dave Pierce: Some of the principles live on, of course, even to the galling realization that Rush Limbaugh is using some of the same techniques that we developed. A few old guys like Laquidara still keep the candle burning, but once in a while you hear a group of Young Turk deejays who are out of the box, wrapped in nineties hip, playing a wide selection of music. In Lafayette, Louisiana, Cool 96 has been pushing the boundaries on music and deejay rap for a couple of years, but there's no social revolution going on, so there is no raison d'être. There's nothing in the music that makes you want to protest and march. Still I keep listening. Occasionally I hear a young, energetic jock put together a great set, and I have to smile.

Larry Miller: I'm not convinced that something akin to underground will never resurface. Digital satellite programming may open up a lot of new venues for a wider variety of radio programming. Less commercial, more room for innovation and creativity. I think every deejay's dream is to do his show from home (a cabin in the woods) and play whatever he likes and make good money doing it. The AM-FM bands are hopelessly bogged down in "marketing," but there is hope. Watch the skies.

Ed Shane: There have been signs. Today's modern rock stations show the same experimental qualities that the commercial underground stations had. They're taking risks with new music. They're having fun with production. They're showing respect for the music by keeping the announcers out of the way. The best of the modern rock stations showcase live bands and provide lots of information about the artists and the music. "Generation X" modern rock stations tend to add a political spin to topics like the environment and the media.

John Gehron: The program directors and on-air talent have many of the underlying ideals of the early progressive stations. They are honest to the music and try not to jive the audience. So remnants of the early stations exist in the approach used to reach Generation X.

Dwight Douglas: Alternative today is the new progressive format. It has all the same elements we saw in the late 1960s. The only difference is debt service, which will always drive expectations too hard.

Al Wilson: To a certain extent, history is repeating itself. The music that represents the nineteen- to thirty-year-old has spawned the alternative format. This format started with stations such as KROQ on Los Angeles and 91X in San Diego, when artists like U2 and the Cure were unknown. It is becoming mainstream very quickly, and again I believe that to be a reflection of today's technology and the rapid pace of social change.

Bonnie Simmons: This stuff like "alternative adult" is not a rebirth of underground, despite all the rhetoric about a return to 1969. I don't see there's a real comparison to be made.

Roland Jacopetti: You know, there's nothing sadder than these "classic rock" stations playing the music that people had psychedelic experiences with or made love with or died in Vietnam with. They're all formatted to the hilt and automated. They extrude from the radio as just another processed product. I always think of e. e. cummings' line, "Comes out like a ribbon, lies flat on the brush."

The possibility of a new distribution modus operandi for commercial underground programming has been raised by a number of people since the heyday of the genre. Notes Ben Fong-Torres:

> Given the paranoia that has so much of the radio industry transfixed and the inevitable boorishness of non-profit, non-directional radio, it would appear that radio will have to find an alternative to the public airwaves, an alternative to corporate or network funding—if it is to succeed in doing its most vital job. That is, relating to, responding to, and serving the immediate community.[28]

Raechel Donahue: The only kind of revolution comparable to underground radio today is on the Internet. People will not go out on the street to create change, so cyberspace is fertile ground, so to speak. Discounting time travel, though, I think it's safe to say it will never be as it was, but then neither will anything else. Wasn't it David Eisenhower who said, "Things are more the same today than they have ever been in the past"? In 1989 Scott Campbell, a.k.a. Freddy Snakeskin, put together a radio station, MARS-FM, that was synonymous with the philosophy of KMPX. It was new music that was selling and that wasn't being played on commercial radio, techno, industrial, and house music—the stuff of raves and underground clubs. It got a lot of national and international press, but it ultimately fell prey to the demands of the corporate beast and died after about a year and a half, leaving college radio to take up the flag.

Thom O'Hair: The one place I think has a chance to generate this level of excitement in broadcast is on the Internet. There will be a day in the not too distant future when the Net will carry many stations, and the programming possibilties are endless and wonderfully varied. How about interactive underground radio?

Dwight Douglas: The Internet is the new FM radio. This is where the future is. Radio will only be a minor event, a convenience store on the information highway.

Larry Soley: College radio stations took over where the undergrounders left off. Then college radio lost it, and it was no longer avant garde. With the demise of that distribution source, the avant garde has shifted to pirate radio stations, particularly micropower stations like Radio Free Ybor City and San Francisco Liberation Radio, which mix political talk and cutting-edge music, very much like the FM stations in the 1960s did. On these stations, the Clash's "This Is Radio Clash" and Billy Bragg's "Which Side Are You On?" are considered "golden oldies." Now, there are "free radio stations"—the preferred term for pirate radio stations—in Berkeley, San Francisco, Tampa, New York, and even smaller cities like Fresno, California, and Decatur, Illinois. These stations blur the distinction between listeners and programmers. A listener can become a disc jockey, announcer, or commentator on these stations. They're what radio was meant to be.

Some diehard freeformers, such as Vin Scelsa on WXRK-FM in New York City, still get airtime. At the station he mixes an eclectic blend of music and does not restrict his conversation to liner-cards. According to an article in the *Wall Street Journal* in late 1991, the freeform format was enjoying a modest comeback, but the article went on to suggest that it is doubtful it will be more widely employed in the future. At the time the piece was published, Scelsa was confined to a few hours on Sunday nights. There are a few instances where former underground radio deejays have resorted to shifts on noncommercial stations to keep their art form alive.

Charles Laquidara: College and public stations provide about the only opportunities currently out there. College is where the underground format is at if it's anywhere at all right now. They can do it, but the commercial radio medium can't.

Roland Jacopetti: I think the only "revival" of underground radio will be, and is, in the college stations. Sometimes an independent commercial flirts with it, but then the corporate bozos come in and chop off its long locks for the sake of the almighty dollar. Even Pacifica Radio, half-century bastion of sensitivity and intelligence on the airwaves, is lately going down the tubes, guided by management that alternately has its nose in the Arbitron books and up its ass. So now I'm listening to tapes on my car radio. I shut off the radio when the news stations assaulted me one too many times with obnoxious ads—my tolerance for ads decreases like my tolerance for second-hand cigarette smoke—and both the Pacifica and NPR stations were broadcasting programs about how to invest your money. Yet, as Lawrence Ferlinghetti put it, "I'm always waiting for a new rebirth of wonder."

Russ Gibb: A lot of college stations are playing real niche music, and it might migrate over in some form to the commercial end of the band.

Tim Powell: I hear a lot at the bottom of the dial that you can't hear anywhere else. FM college stations still play Archie Shepp next to Nine Inch Nails. There's no market on commercial FM because there's no real youth bulge. Radio programmers have deadened the ears of my generation, otherwise radio wouldn't be such a nostalgic avalanche of melancholia occasionally brightened by some prescribed patter from someone who has learned to sound interested even if bored to tears.

Dan Carlisle: For me, college radio is a pale example of what we did, but it does offer a similar ethic. Listening to the new Triple A format, like at KFOG in San Francisco, I'd say it doesn't. Having worked this format, I found it very repetitive and bland. I still believe in the original plan. Build a great station and the listeners will come.

Thom O'Hair: The big question to me is, after a quarter of a century, why isn't there a noncommercial station that is near the top of the ratings in a major market? Why does everybody think that if a station is commercial it can't have some good points and effect positive change? I'll grant you that most of them do not, but the fact is most noncoms don't either. Take almost any multi-station market and scan the left side of the FM dial. The stations are all doing the same thing. Just how many times and on how many stations does the listener want to hear "Small Things Considered" and "Boring Edition," then a little classical music, a smattering of jazz and ethnic, and the cycle is repeated ad nauseum. When I ask program directors why, they all say about the same thing—they do it for the money. During pledge week, those are the shows that supporters pledge to, they respond. If the show doesn't raise money, it's gone. Kind of like the commercial world, isn't it?

SPINNING THE ALTERNATIVE

Like a wheel within a wheel.

In the mid-1990s radio programming maestro Lee Abrams was at work on the creation of a new format that would tap the disenfranchised baby-boomer audience. The following memorandum to his network hierarchy summarizes his concept.

For several months, I've been watching and working on a potential Adult Alternative format—also referred to as AAA or Adult Progressive. Per David K., I'd appreciate feedback on the potential of this concept, to see if we should move ahead. Here is an overview:

— The target audience is 30–49. It's really a sophisticated AOR station. Z-Rock is young, Classic Rock is middle age, AAA is upper end in terms of audience demos and musical sophistication. Ideally, this format would give us excellent coverage of the Rock demographic spectrum.

— There's a good buzz on this concept. The highly suspect *Radio Only* claims it's the fastest growing music format.

— Definitely a major market sell.

— There is a large generation of people who have been into AOR since the late '60's. This format is geared to reach these listeners. This is the kind of format New-FM should do.

— Existing AAA stations include WXRT/Chicago, KBCO/Denver, KFOG/San Francisco, and WBOS/Boston. Though I don't think any of these stations are doing a synicatably good job at it. While not given the credit, WMMO in Orlando was actually an early force in AAA.

— Typical artists range from people like the Beatles, Peter Gabriel, Hendrix, and Clapton, and there is also room for the more eclectic types such as Van Morrison and Enya. The musical idea is popular eclectic. It's a place a 40 year old AOR rooted person can go without hearing "Light My Fire" again.

— From a programming standpoint, I believe we could quickly develop an outstanding sounding format that could become the standard for this approach. One of the key selling points would be the perceived qualitative superiority, much like the better marketed New Adult Contemporary stations enjoy.

— While there's a buzz on '70's music out there, my gut says that this proposed format will be even more attractive in the mid-1990's.

Your feedback on the viability of this concept is requested and appreciated.

THOSE WERE THE STATIONS—FLASHBACKS IN THE UNDERGROUND

Life is a series of moments, man, that you dig while they're happening and don't expect to constantly repeat them.[29]

—Tom Donahue

The "Voices" featured in this book were asked to convey their personal choices for best underground station(s) and on-air personality or personalities. Not all cared to respond, indicating that they were unwilling to engage in any form of rankings or ratings game—which, in the end, was antithetical to the very nature of what these stations and they themselves sought to represent. Many former underground employees who were contacted for their views were disinclined to be counted among their past colleagues in an attempt to avoid further compounding the negative stigma they feel their involvement in the programming genre has inspired.

Further studies on this topic will be conducted and published at a future date. The author encourages readers to submit their own views and comments for possible inclusion. Mail to the author, c/o Boston College, Chestnut Hill, Massachusetts 02167.

Ed Shane: I had a particular affinity for WABX in Detroit, probably because I was exposed to it on a regular basis. Of course, I happen to think my own station, WPLO, sounded quite good.

Dave Pierce: The premier stations from my perspective were KPPC from the church basement in Pasadena (talk about literally underground), KMPX up north, and WBCN on the East Coast. KSAN and KMET were too corporate in their structure to be really pure underground.

Dan Carlisle: For my money, the model for underground was WABX-FM. Not the first of its kind but certainly to be counted among the elite top five in this category. This was a pure Midwest product created by natives. The players all came from strong commercial backgrounds. We knew what we didn't like. While there was certainly a station sound, each full-time member seemed to be strong where another was weak. Dave Dixon was strong in folk, having written "I Dig Rock and Roll Music" for Peter, Paul and Mary. I was big with the loud stuff, and so on. We could write and produce commercials and relished our time in the production room. We knew how important it was to match the commercials with the air sound. As a staff, we produced an ongoing daily drama serial. Sunday we acted out the comics. WABX created seasonal traditions, such as the Spring Kite-In, free concerts in the park. The station was the campfire you could gather around to hear the new music and information about the counterculture. Besides my obvious preference for best underground station, there were others I admired and respected. For example, WMMR/Philadelphia, WNEW/New York, WBCN/Boston, WMMS/Cleveland, and, of course, KSAN/San Francisco.

Al Wilson: The stations that represented that generation of people the best in their respective areas, for me, include KMET, WABX, WBCN, KSAN, WNEW, and WXRT. They were excellent at what they did.

Tim Powell: WBCN serves as a good model of this kind of station. WMMS in Cleveland was solid within the context of what a whupped-ass, rust belt mess that city was. WABX was good or bad depending on the jock. KPPC was fine at times.

Kate Ingram: KSAN and WBCN really defined the format in the 1970s. They influenced so many others.

Frank Wood: I'd have to go with WEBN-FM as the best example of this kind of radio, and I'd offer Denton Marr as the finest underground airman.

Dwight Douglas: I traveled a lot when I was young, so I actually heard many of the big undergrounds. Here are my best main cuts: WNEW-FM (with Rosco and Jonathan

Schwartz), WBCN (with Charles Laquidara), CHOM-FM in Montreal (aired in two languages), Tom Donahue (wherever he was and whatever he did), KSAN (with Tony Pigg), KMET (with its stellar music), WMMR (with its exceptional production), WLAV (old stalwart freeformer). These stations all seemed to possess something special, a personal style, which was thread[ed] through every show.

Raechel Donahue: Well, it won't surprise anyone that my personal favorites are KMPX and KSAN. We created the mold for the format. As far as the best underground personality, it will come as no surprise that I cast my ballot for Tom Donahue. He used to call himself the forty-seven-year-old Perfect Master, and anyone who's heard him would agree. Bill Graham said Tom had a voice like Zeus, and Tom considered himself the ultimate groupie. Of course, there were other great jocks from the era. Steven Segal—The Obscene Steven Clean—was one. He wandered into the station from the street barefoot, and Tom put him on the air. He could turn a three-line psa into a two-minute work of art, but he couldn't read a straight spot to save his twisted soul. He wasn't all that professional, but listening to him was like watching a tightrope walker. Thom O'Hair was the consummate pro—almost too terse sometimes—but he could make the coolest segues. B. Mitchel Reed was the elder statesman of the group. He was the first Top 40 deejay to join Tom's club. I think the smoothest of them all was Dusty Street, the first female in this format. She had a great deal of knowledge of blues and R&B and a voice so husky it could have been pulling a sled. She went on to the next step when underground folded, joining alternative KROQ in its fledgling days. She's the only one left on the air to my knowledge—a legend in her own time.

Lee Abrams: The stations that epitomized the movement for me and were models of this format were KSAN and KMPX. They're first and foremost.

John Gehron: I'd have to go on record as saying that the best underground stations were KSAN, WXRT, WNEW, and WMMR. They were the undisputed pioneers. They had the beliefs and held on to them longer than the others.

Shelley Grafman: The stations of that time period which best exemplified the whole progressive, freeform rock action were KSHE, WABX, WBCN, KMET, and WMMS. There will never be stations like these—doing what they did—again, in my opinion.

Russ Gibb: My vote goes first to WKMH, and WABX, which took over where the former left off.

Dusty Street: These stations were very individual, so it's like ranking something very human. Speaking of classifying things, which is something I generally avoid, many of the jocks from underground have been stigmatized by their involvement in the format. There is a level of discrimination, or shall we say bias, against those who worked at these stations. We've been labeled as something weird—too weird to deal with. We're those crazies from the hippie radio days. Maybe there's some truth to it, but there's an awful lot of great talent going to waste. Of course, we're all getting so damn old, maybe it's age discrimination.

Raechel Donahue: There are an awful lot of underground folk out of the business and even out of work. This is due to a warped perception of these people. You know, "those freaks from radical radio." Most undergrounders are out of the business. There are one or two exceptions, but that's about it.

Dan Carlisle: Today many of the former tribe complain of the lack of opportunities for them in the radio marketplace. There is a patina attached to many of us who worked at underground stations. The industry itself has the notion that if you worked in that arena, you were a pothead then, so you must be a pothead now.

Raechel Donahue: You don't mind being damned for the sins of your past, but when you're damned for trying to be innovative and make a contribution, well . . .

Stefan Ponek: After a long hiatus from radio, I returned in 1991. I stumbled into a suburban AM daytimer near where I live and turned it around for the new owners. Not long after, I headed to Northern California and did likewise for the same investor group. I enjoyed the hell out of it until the investors backed off for unrelated reasons and I took a buyoff to ease the drain. Business is business is business. Some things don't change, whereas other things change completely. If anybody showed up stoned at any of our stations today, I'd can them in a hot second. How about that?

May each and every one of you find a little pot at the end of your rainbow.

—Larry Miller's daily radio program sign-off

Radio is a powerful medium. Those who work in it must fall in love again, generate passion for their work, and have pride in quality programming.

—Paul Carroll, *Broadcasting and Cable*, July 22, 1996

NOTES

1. Richard Goldstein, *Reporting the Counterculture* (New York: Unwin Hyman, 1989), p. xix.

2. Bob Guccione, Jr., "A Commentary," *Los Angeles Times*, August 14, 1994, p. 5.

3. Joshua Mills, "Media," *New York Times*, June 19, 1995, p. D7.

4. *Life*, December 1969, p. 114.

5. Peter Fornatale and Joshua Mills, *Radio in the Television Age* (New York: Doubleday, 1969), p. 135.

6. Ben Fong-Torres, "FM Underground Radio: Love for Sale," *Rolling Stone*, April 2, 1970, p. 6.

7. Annie Gottlieb, *Do You Believe in Magic?* (New York: Times Books, 1987), p. 195.

8. *Variety*, April 5, 1972, p. 7.

9. David Caute, *The Year of the Barricades: A Journey Through 1968* (New York: Harper and Row, 1988), p. xiii.

10. Theodore Roszak, *The Making of the Counter Culture* (New York: Doubleday, 1969), p. 193.

11. Rex Weiner, *Commentary*, 1972, p. 8.

12. Lynda Crawford, "Underground Radio," *East Village Other*, 1971, p. 11.

13. Susan Krieger, *Hip Capitalism* (Hollywood: Sage Publications, 1979), p. 121.

14. Ibid., p. 289.

15. Fong-Torres, "FM Underground Radio: Love for Sale," p. 8.

16. Carl LaFong, "Notes from the Underground," *Record World*, August 20, 1969, p. 11.

17. *Variety*, July 8, 1970.

18. Marc Eliot, *Rockonomics: The Money Behind the Music* (New York: Carol Publishing, 1993), p. 71.

19. Peter Knobler, *Zygote*, May 1, 1971, p. 9.

20. *Atlantic Newsletter*, February 16, 1971, p. 2.

21. "Progressive Rock," *Broadcasting*, September 24, 1973, p. 36.

22. Steve Post, "Son of Play List: The Decline and Fall of Commercial Free Form Radio," *Village Voice*, October 14, 1971, p. 49.

23. Ibid., p. 60.

24. *Walrus*, November 24, 1971, p. 5.

25. John J. O'Connor, "FM Radio's Ear to the Underground," *Wall Street Journal*, August 27, 1970.

26. *Village Voice*, October 14, 1971, p. 61.

27. *Walrus*, November 24, 1971, p. 2.

28. Fong-Torres, "FM Underground Radio: Love for Sale," p. 8.

29. Quoted in Krieger, *Hip Capitalism*, p. 270.

Underground Radio Stations

The following commercial radio stations identified them-selves as either underground, progressive, or freeform on a full- or part-time basis in the late 1960s and early 1970s.

Alabama

WAQY-AM	Birmingham

Arizona

KDBK-AM	Mesa

Arkansas

KZRK-AM	Ozark

California

KXGO-FM	Arcata
KPAT-FM	Berkeley
KRE-AM	Berkeley
KLRB-FM	Carmel
KFIG-FM	Fresno
KUNF-AM	La Canada
KLOS-FM	Los Angeles
KWST-FM	Los Angeles
KLBS-FM	Los Banos
KDHS-FM	Modesto
KEDC-FM	Northridge
KPPC-FM	Pasadena
KCRA-AM	Sacramento
KSFM-FM	Sacramento
KZAP-FM	Sacramento
KPRI-FM	San Diego
KIOI-FM	San Francisco
KMEL-FM	San Francisco
KOIT-FM	San Francisco
KSAN-FM	San Francisco
KSFX-FM	San Francisco
KOME-FM	San Jose
KTYD-FM	Santa Barbara

Colorado

KKFM-FM	Colorado Springs
KBPI-FM	Denver

Connecticut

WHCN-FM	Hartford
WYBC-FM	New Haven

Source: Broadcasting Yearbook (1967–1972).

Florida

WGVL-FM	Gainesville
WAIV-FM	Jacksonville
WBUS-FM	Miami Beach
WORJ-FM	Orlando
WMAI-FM	Panama City

Georgia

WDEC-AM	Americus
WDOL-FM	Athens
WMRE-AM	Monroe
WSOK-AM	Savannah

Hawaii

KHAI-FM	Honolulu

Illinois

WDAI-FM	Chicago
WKQK-FM	Chicago
WSDN-FM	Chicago
WGHS-FM	Glen Ellyn
WINU-FM	Highland
WKAI-FM	Macomb

Iowa

KFMG-FM	Des Moines

Kansas

KUPK-AM	Garden City
KMAN-FM	Manhattan

Kentucky

WKRX-FM	Louisville
WLRS-FM	Louisville

Louisiana

WRNO-FM	New Orleans

Maryland

WAYE-AM	Baltimore
WKTK-FM	Catonsville
WINX-AM	Rockville

Massachusetts

WBCN-FM	Boston
WCOZ-FM	Boston
WCAS-AM	Cambridge
WCFN-FM	Williamstown
WAAF-FM	Worcester

Michigan

WNRZ-FM	Ann Arbor
WABX-FM	Detroit
WRIX-FM	Detroit
WWWW-FM	Detroit

Minnesota

KQRS-AM	Golden Valley

Missouri

KSOZ-FM	Fort Lookout
KYYS-FM	Kansas City
KSHE-FM	St. Louis

Montana

KXGN-AM	Glendive

Nebraska

KFMQ-AM	Lincoln

New Jersey

WPRB-FM	Princeton

New Mexico

KRST-FM	Albuquerque
KKAT-AM	Roswell

New York

WLIR-FM	Garden City
WVBR-FM	Ithaca
WNEW-FM	New York
WPLJ-FM	New York
WCMF-AM	Rochester
WIRQ-FM	Rochester
WGY-AM	Schnectady

WOUR-FM	Utica	KSTI-FM	Springfield

North Carolina

		Tennessee	
WRNA-FM	Charlotte	WROL-AM	Knoxville
WDMS-FM	Durham	WMC-FM	Memphis
		WKDA-FM	Nashville

Ohio

WAUP-FM	Akron	**Texas**	
WEBN-FM	Cincinnati	KAMC-FM	Arlington
WMMS-FM	Cleveland	KFMF-FM	Corpus Christi
WNCR-FM	Cleveland	KFWD-FM	Dallas
WLMJ-FM	Jackson	KNUS-FM	Dallas
WQXR-FM	Oxford	KRLD-FM	Dallas

Oklahoma

		KIXY-FM	San Angelo
KMOD-FM	Tulsa	KSHN-FM	Sherman

Oregon

		KYLE-FM	Temple
KZEL-FM	Eugene		

Utah

Pennsylvania

		KVNU-AM	Logan
WSAN-AM	Allentown		
WCRO-AM	Johnstown	**Virginia**	
WIFI-FM	Philadelphia	WXRI-FM	Norfolk
WMMR-FM	Philadelphia		
WDVE-FM	Pittsburgh	**Washington**	
WYDD-FM	Pittsburgh	KJR-FM	Seattle
WRHY-FM	Starview	KOL-FM	Seattle
WQWK-AM	State College	KZOK-FM	Seattle
		KLAY-FM	Tacoma

Rhode Island

		KTAC-FM	Tacoma
WBRU-FM	Providence		

South Dakota

		Wisconsin	
KESD-FM	Brookings	WIBA-FM	Madison

Appendix B

The History of Album Rock Radio According to Lee Abrams

One of radio's most successful programmers provides his take on the evolution of album rock radio. In 1996 Abrams left ABC Radio to work as an independent programming consultant.

1968–1970: UTOPIAN RADIO. Total jock freedom. Stations were practically tools of the New Left. Advertisers were pigs. Drug price reports followed the news.

1971–1973: EARLY ALBUM ORIENTED ROCK (AOR). Underground Utopian stations were suddenly challenged by newcomers, who treated album cuts with Top 40 sensibility. Familiarity and a political stance opened up cume beyond hippies.

1974–1976: AOR GETS RESPECT. Underground radio died from self-inflicted elitism and musical self-indulgence, while AORs started to establish real consistent 12–24 [age group] numbers. Major group operators, like Taft, Plough, and ABC, embraced the format. Some advertiser resistance, but profits were improving. Cheap to run.

1977–1978: PUNK/DISCO ERA. AOR music was attacked from two sides, English Punk and New York Disco. Stations that integrated those forms got hurt. Music press declared AOR dead, but the audience hated disco and punk, and straight-ahead AORs flourished.

1979–1980: MODEL ERA. This meant picking a mode of music—in this case, hard rock—and reestablishing AOR as "rock 'n' roll." Never again was Carly Simon, James Taylor, or Carol King heard on AOR. It was now Heart, Journey, Foreigner, and Ted Nugent. Stations burned disco records on the air and adapted "street" logos and attitude. Massively successful. Ratings soared.

1981–1982: CLEARLY BETTER ERA. Scores of new consultants and call-out researchers put pressure on dominant AORs to outperform competitors. Many new AORs join the format. Many class AOR battles. Sleeping AORs got caught. Heat was on to "Be clearly better" than the competition.

1983: NEW MUSIC. New bands were abundant. Some worked AOR (U2 and the Police). Others were a disaster (Haircut 100 and Flock of Seagulls). A dangerous era because the new album artists had questionable rock 'n' roll roots and integrity. They also had suspicious haircuts (to the audience). The "How do we deal with MTV" question was hot.

1984: 25–44 REALITY. AORs came to a universal conclusion that the 12–24 year old audience was truly growing up with AOR and that the future was in the 25 plus "heritage" listeners. Stations were very cautious with newer bands and hard-edged material—regardless of sales—and focused on heritage and classic artists and 25 plus friendly presentation.

1987–1990: OFFENSE. More AORs started getting aggressive with marketing, "causes," and promotional profiles. Certain jocks have by now established themselves as major personalities.

1991: PICK TURF. As AORs generally solidified their 25 plus turf, a giant hole appears in the younger end as hard-edged bands dominate charts and audiences. Reaction is a new generation of AOR-inspired formats, like Z-Rock, Outlaw Radio, etc. AOR-based stations need to pick turf-battle on the upper end or establish a foothold on the younger end (both being difficult to reach simultaneously).

In the mid-1990s, Abrams proposed a more honed alternative format intended to attract a segment of the baby-boomer listening audience, which had become increasingly frustrated with the absence of meaningful programming on the FM band.

Further Reading

Anderson, Mary Siler. *What Ever Happened to the Hippies?* San Pedro, CA: R & E Miles, 1990.

Barnouw, Erik. *The Image Empire: The History of Broadcasting in the United States, from 1953.* New York: Oxford University Press, 1970.

Berger, Bennett M. *The Survival of the Counterculture.* Berkeley: University of California Press, 1981.

Berman, Paul. *A Tale of Two Utopias.* New York: W. W. Norton, 1996.

Bockris, Victor. *Lou Reed: The Biography.* London: Vintage, 1994.

Cleaver, Eldridge. *Soul on Ice.* New York: McGraw-Hill, 1967.

DCC Compact Classics. "The Golden Age of Underground Radio." Recording, 1989.

Farber, David R. *The Age of Great Dreams.* New York: Hill and Wang, 1994.

Flack, Audrey. *Breaking the Rules.* New York: Abrams, 1992.

Gardner, Richard. *Alternative America.* Cambridge, MA: Gardner, 1995.

Give Peace a Chance: Exploring the Vietnam Antiwar Movement. Charles De-Benedetti Memorial Conference. Syracuse, NY: Syracuse University Press, 1992.

Gorg, Alan. *The Sixties.* Marina Del Ray, CA: Media Associates, 1995.

Goulden, Joseph C. *The Best Years: 1945–1950.* New York: Atheneum, 1976.

Gross, Henry. *The Flower People.* New York: Ballantine Books, 1968.

Guinness, Os. *The Sixties Counterculture and How It Changed America.* Wheaton, IL: Crossway Books, 1994.

Hayden, Tom. *Reunion: A Memoir.* London: Hamilton, 1989.

Henderson, David. *'Scuse Me While I Kiss the Sky.* New York: Bantam Books, 1996.

Hilliard, Robert L., and Michael C. Keith. *The Broadcast Century.* 2nd ed. Boston: Focal Press, 1997.

Hoffman, Abbie. *Steal This Book.* New York: Grove Press, 1971.

Horowitz, David. *Counterculture and Revolution.* New York: Random House, 1972.

Hubner, John. *Bottom Feeders: From Free Love to Hard Core.* New York: Dell, 1994.

Kaiser, Charles. *1968 in America.* New York: Weidenfeld and Nicolson, 1988.

Keith, Michael C. *Radio Programming: Consultancy and Formatics.* Boston: Focal Press, 1987.

King, Mary. *Freedom Song.* New York: Morrow, 1987.

Laffan, Barry. *Communal Organization and Social Transition.* New York: P. Lang, 1996.

Leary, Timothy. *Flashbacks.* New York: St. Martin's Press, 1990.

Lichty, Lawrence W., and Malachi C. Topping. *American Broadcasting: A Sourcebook on the History of Radio and Television.* New York: Hastings House, 1975.

MacFarland, David T. *The Development of the Top 40 Format.* New York: Arno Press, 1979.

Mailer, Norman. *The Armies of the Night.* New York: Signet, 1968.

Mason, Lisa. *Summer of Love.* New York: Bantam Books, 1994.

Matusow, Allen J. *The Unraveling of America.* New York: Harper and Row, 1984.

Mitchell, Jack M. *Great American, Mind-Blowing, Underground Catalog.* San Diego: MSW Enterprises, 1973.

Perry, Paul. *On the Bus.* London: Plexus, 1991.

Pirsig, Robert M. *Zen and the Art of Motorcycle Maintenance.* New York: William Morrow, 1974.

Roszak, Theodore. *Where the Wasteland Ends.* New York: Doubleday, 1972.

Rubin, Jerry. *We Are Everywhere,* New York: Harper and Row, 1971.

Sklar, Rick. *Rocking America.* New York: St. Martin's Press, 1984.

Soley, Lawrence. *Free Radio Broadcasting.* Boston: South End Press, forthcoming.

Spatori, William Charles. *Here Come the Hippies.* Hollywood, CA: Brandon House, 1967.

Thompson, Hunter S. *Fear and Loathing in Las Vegas.* New York: Warner Books, 1971.

Tipton, Steven M. *Getting Saved from the Sixties.* Berkeley: University of California Press, 1982.

Unger, Irwin. *America in the 1960's.* New York: Brandywine Press, 1988.

Voder, Andrew R. *Pirate Radio.* Solana Beach, CA: HighText, 1996.

Von Hoffman, Nicholas. *We Are the People Our Parents Warned Us Against.* Chicago: Ivan Dee, 1968.

Wakefield, Michael P. *In Empty Time and Empty Space.* Chapel Hill: University of North Carolina Press, 1994.

Whitmer, Peter O. *Aquarius Revisited.* New York: Citadel Press, 1991.

Windt, Theodore. *Presidents and Protesters*. Tuscaloosa: University of Alabama Press, 1990.

Wolfe, Tom. *The Electric Kool-Aid Acid Test*. New York: Bantam Books, 1968.

———. *Radical Chic and Mau-Mauing the Flak Catchers*. New York: Noonday Press, 1970.

Index

About the Author

MICHAEL C. KEITH is a professor of Communication at Boston College. He is the author of several books on the electronic media, including *The Radio Station, The Broadcast Century*, and *Signals in the Air: Native American Broadcasting* (Praeger, 1995). He has held various positions at colleges and radio stations, and was Chair of Education at the Museum of Broadcast Communications.

About the Author

MICHAEL C. KEITH is a professor of Communication at Boston College. He is the author of several books on the electronic media, including *The Radio Station, The Broadcast Century*, and *Signals in the Air: Native American Broadcasting* (Praeger, 1995). He has held various positions at colleges and radio stations, and was Chair of Education at the Museum of Broadcast Communications.